CPE FIELD GUIDE

The Definitive Operations Manual for Developers of Training for CPAs

CPE FIELD GUIDE

The Definitive Operations Manual for
Developers of Training for CPAs

GROUP-LIVE VERSION

Ross Stern ◆ Rod Mebane

St. Charles Publications

An activity of the St. Charles Consulting Group

St. Charles, Illinois

Ross Stern ◆ Rod Mebane
CPE Field Guide: The Definitive Operations Manual for Developers of Training for CPAs
(GROUP-LIVE VERSION)
St. Charles, Illinois / St. Charles Publications / 2010
104 pp / ISBN 978-0-9826633-0-1

Cover design and internal illustrations by Tracy Garner of Long Beach, California

The **CPE Field Guide** is not endorsed by the American Institute of Certified Public Accountants (AICPA), the National Association of State Boards of Accountancy (NASBA), or any public regulatory body. While extensive effort has been applied to ensure the accuracy of the information contained in this book, it is a dynamic environment, and no guarantees are offered. If there are any questions about accuracy or completeness, readers should contact the responsible regulatory or rule-setting group.

The authors would like the **CPE Field Guide** to be a "living" document and to become increasingly meaningful and comprehensive for CPE planners over time. Readers are invited to critique what is here, to suggest changes, and to offer ideas for additional topics to be addressed.

14 13 12 11 10   10 9 8 7 6 5 4 3 2 1

St. Charles Publications
An activity of the St. Charles Consulting Group

1121 East Main Street, Suite 220
St. Charles, Illinois 60174
United States of America

PUBLISHER@STCHARLESPUBLICATIONS.COM

DEDICATION

The authors of the **CPE Field Guide** dedicate this book to:

Phil Davis and **Bob Hiebeler**
– the founding partners of the St. Charles Consulting Group –

for the qualities that have made the firm the successful enterprise that it is today:
vision, passion, creativity, dedication, tenacity, and good humor.

St.Charles
Consulting Group

CPE FIELD GUIDE

Contents

Introduction

Those responsible for or involved with the creation of training programs that satisfy the standards for Continuing Professional Education (CPE) for CPAs are generally people, in our opinion, who should be highly regarded. For many, CPE involvement is just a part of a larger set of demanding job responsibilities. The work is often challenged by tight budgets and tight timelines. Often the subject matter of training is technical and complex, requiring the involvement of subject matter experts who are line professionals whose first priority is client work. Moreover, the audience of CPAs and other finance & consulting professionals is often demanding in terms of how their time is spent in a training session. All of these things add up to a difficult job and, on top of these environmental demands, there is a whole set of CPE rules that need to be followed, which are not always clearly laid out and tend to seem a bit confusing and at times overwhelming.

The **CPE Field Guide** is a highly niched publication aimed specifically at these people – creators of CPE for CPAs. Those of you old enough to remember Johnny Carson (host of *The Tonight Show* before Jay Leno took over ... the first time) will recall Ed McMahon, Johnny Carson's long-time late-night sidekick. Ed had a bit when he would say, "EVERYTHING you needed to know about something is contained in this book," to which Johnny would reply, "Au contraire, mon frère." While we are not claiming that the **CPE Field Guide** covers EVERYTHING one might need to know about meeting the standards for CPE, it provides a great foundation and will answer the most critical questions that anxious professionals charged with CPE responsibilities might need to know. We see the challenge of meeting the standards as at times a battle, and our intent is to help people navigate through the trenches and meet the challenge with a minimum amount of inefficiency, inaccuracy, and frustration. The "battle" concept is what gave rise to the notion of reflecting a "guerilla" type theme that you see on the cover.

Establishing the credentials for a CPE-qualified program is both an art and a science. There are clearly defined rules on how to document a program so that it meets the CPE standards, but the groundwork for meeting those standards is done during the define, design, develop, and deliver phases of a project. These phases, when well executed, form the spine of every successful training intervention. This **CPE Field Guide** provides helpful tips, tools, and templates for each phase that cover the basics of good course design, and it is written in a way that non-training professionals can easily follow and apply. Using the resources contained in this book, you can have greater confidence that the finished training product will both accomplish your training objectives and meet the necessary qualifications for CPE credit.

Our fundamental interest at the St. Charles Consulting Group is effectiveness of learning. While of course it is necessary for CPAs to get their CPE credits, there is sometimes a tendency to sacrifice quality in favor of expediency – and those in the business can recall all too many sessions where a boring, monotonous technical expert, with text-laden slides, labors on about some minutiae associated a new technical pronouncement. Not quality education, but good enough for CPE. Our hope is that, by streamlining the CPE aspects of program development, more attention can be paid to the quality of the educational content and program delivery so that what people take out of the program is timely, accurate, relevant, and applicable to the work.

We hope you find the **CPE Field Guide** useful and encourage you to share your reactions and suggestions.

Ross Stern ◆ Rod Mebane
St. Charles, Illinois – September 2010

How to Use This Book

Most Certified Public Accountants (CPAs) are regularly required to take a certain amount of Continuing Professional Education (CPE) in order to maintain their CPA licenses, and there are quality standards that providers of CPE programs need to meet in order for their programs to count toward the CPE requirements. The **CPE Field Guide** is written to help those responsible for creating CPE programs satisfy the quality standards <u>and</u> provide valuable training experiences.

This book has no fluff or frills. It is practical. It is tactical. It is pragmatic and hands-on. In fact, the **CPE Field Guide** is better thought of as a toolbox than a book. It is complete with 46 different tools, organized according to the "5D" model that the St. Charles Consulting Group uses to chart the development of training programs from start to finish, with phases that include: **D**efine, **D**esign, **D**evelop, **D**eliver, and **D**ocument. For easy reference, each tool in the box is referred to by a phase name and a tool number, e.g., Design T-04 refers to the "Working with Subject Matter Experts" tool.

In many respects, guidance in the **CPE Field Guide** is applicable to any training situation. But, as suggested, the accounting profession is held to a higher standard than many others. It is important to state regulatory bodies that those who are given the CPA designation regularly take courses to maintain and improve their professional competence, and they set standards to ensure that the quality of instruction is sound. In general, the standards are sensible and consistent with prudent instructional design practices but, by codifying and enforcing the standards, there is greater consistency and generally higher quality in the educational content.

Regulatory bodies that come into play include the various state boards of accountancy, the Public Company Accounting Oversight Board (PCAOB), the Government Accountability Office (GAO), and the Employee Benefit Plan Audit Quality Center, and theoretically they could all have different standards. However, to streamline matters somewhat, the American Institute of Certified Public Accountants (AICPA) has teamed with the National Association of State Boards of Accountancy (NASBA) to promulgate a common set of CPE rules. The most recent standards were issued in 2002, and they are now recognized in some respect by virtually all states and territories.

The joint AICPA/NASBA "Statement on Standards for Continuing Professional Education (CPE) Programs," on which much of the **CPE Field Guide** relies, can be found on the NASBA website (WWW.NASBA.ORG). Other important sources of CPE-related information include: NASBA's "CPE Program Sponsor Requirements " and "FAQs for CPE," the "Quality Assurance Service (QAS) Sponsor Application," and websites of boards of accountancy in states that have variations on the national CPE standards.

To provide an overview of this CPE toolbox, the various resources included in the **CPE Field Guide** are discussed briefly below, organized along the lines of the St. Charles "5D" (five-phase) process for CPE program creation.

DEFINE

During the definition phase, the high-level project parameters are established. It begins with assessment of the need – what are the overall business objectives and what changes in knowledge and behavior are required in order to satisfy those objectives. The **Needs Assessment Tool** (Define T-01, page 1) will help guide this effort. Once the needs are determined, it is always appropriate to ask if training is the solution or whether non-training solutions might be more effective. The **Non-Training Solutions Tool** (Define T-02, page 3) will help answer these questions. Assuming that the decision is made to go forward with a CPE training program, it is important to get a better sense of the target audience, and that is what the **Audience Analysis Tool** (Define T-03, page 4) is designed to do.

A critical decision in putting together a CPE program relates to the delivery methods that are chosen, and certain methods are more effective in different situations. The **Delivery Strategy Comparison Tool** (Define T-04, page 5) sheds light on those considerations. The next tool – the **Learning Resource Search Tool** (Define T-05, page 8) – provides guidance on where to find relevant information to include in the program. Lastly, if a decision is made to use content that is developed by an external provider, the **Vendor Interview Protocol** (Define T-06, page 9) provides a list of useful questions to ask.

DESIGN

The design phase results in a detailed blueprint for building out the CPE program. We begin this section with the **Project Management Tool** (Design T-01, page 11). Even though this tool spans the entire process, it is very helpful in providing a "big picture" view and in instilling discipline from the early stages of the course creation activity. (Note that there are project steps related to <u>instructional content</u> as well as to <u>administration & logistics</u>.) The following tool – the **Business Plan Document Template** (Design T-02, page 14) – also paints a "big picture" but, in this case, it is more about the business case than about the development process. It is a very useful profile document to share with program sponsors and other interested stakeholders.

It is generally useful to schedule a design meeting at the outset of the project, and the **Design Meeting Planning Tool** (Design T-03, page 16) provides some suggestions along with a sample agenda. Once the work begins, there will often be involvement of subject matter experts (SMEs) to provide the underlying content for the CPE program. It is important that the relationship with SMEs be managed well, and the **Working with Subject Matter Experts** tool (Design T-04, page 17) provides some good advice.

The program design typically begins with a content outline and, accordingly, a **Content Outline Tool** (Design T-05, page 18) is provided to facilitate a useful brainstorming process. This is followed by a **Learning Objectives Writing Guide** (Design T-06, page 19) and an **ABC Learning Objectives Worksheet** (Design T-07, page 20). Both of these are very helpful in thinking through what learning really needs to occur as a result of this program. Learning objectives are core to the entire endeavor. Once these are set, the designer can then consider different learning methods – a process supported by the **Learning Activity Menu** (Design T-08, page 21). We have also included an **ID Theory to Practice Tool** (Design T-09, page 28) to aid designers with ideas for increasing the effectiveness of learning.

This section closes with tools to create two very important design documents – the **CPE Course Description Tool** (Design T-10, page 30) and the **Master Design Document Template** (Design T-11, page 31). The Course Description includes all of the elements that are required by the AICPA/NASBA CPE standards, and the Master Design Document is the blueprint that will guide the work of the program developers.

DEVELOP

Development is where the course construction work takes place. The first tool is simply a form to document the contributors – the **Development Team Profile** (Develop T-01, page 33). CPE standards want to ensure that the team has the right qualifications. The second tool is the **Learning Materials Menu** (Develop T-02, page 34), which provides a checklist of items – the "deliverables" – that might be prepared to support the program. The next items provide guidance on developing certain components of the program: **Creating Scenarios and Role-Plays** (Develop T-03, page 38), **Job Aid on Creating Job Aids** (Develop T-04, page 39), and **Creating Test Items** (Develop T-05, page 40). There is also a brief **Writing Style Guide** (Develop T-06, page 44) and information on **Brand, Copyright and Trademark Guidelines** (Develop T-07, page 46).

The **Quality Assurance Checklist** (Develop T-08, page 47) that follows serves as an excellent list of program success factors. Then there is a form – the **Developer Review Form** (Develop T-09, page 50) – to confirm that the program development process satisfied CPE standards and, since there is a requirement that the material be reviewed by one or more qualified individuals who were <u>not</u> part of the development team, we also include a **Technical Review Form** (Develop T-10, page 51).

If a pilot of the program is conducted – always a good idea – you might want to use the **Pilot Test Observation Checklist** (Develop T-11, page 52) in helping to identify areas where improvements need to be made.

The last two items in the Development section relate to CPE credits. The **CPE Calculation Template** (Develop T-12, page 54), as the name suggests, provides a format for determining the number of CPE credits that should be granted to participants. And, since CPE credits need to be expressed in relation to the appropriate fields of study, a <u>Field of Study Reference Guide</u> (Develop T-13, page 55) is provided.

DELIVER

The CPE program is built and is now ready to be delivered. The section begins with an **Instructor Team Profile** (Deliver T-01, page 57) to capture needed information. The section ends with a sample **CPE Attendance Record** (Deliver T-07, page 66) that can be used to capture participant information.

In between these, we have included a number of tools to serve as resources for instructors to enhance their effectiveness:

- **Instructor Tip Sheet** (Deliver T-02, page 58)
- **Organizing Instructional Activities** (Deliver T-03, page 61)
- **Helping Participants Learn To Learn** (Deliver T-04, page 62)
- **Feedback Guidelines** (Deliver T-05, page 63)
- **Energizers for the Classroom** (Deliver T-06, page 64)

DOCUMENT

At the conclusion of a CPE program, a number of actions need to be completed in the form of collecting, organizing, and storing information in order to create a permanent record of documentation. The tools included here are straightforward:

- The **Participant Evaluation Form** (Document T-01, page 67) and the **Instructor Evaluation Form** (Document T-02, page 68) are used to capture the perspectives of participants and instructors on various aspects of the program.
- A **Participant CPE Certificate Template** (Document T-03, page 69) is used to print certificates evidencing satisfactory completion.
- An **Instructor CPE Submittal Form** (Document T-04, page 70) and an **Instructor CPE Certificate Template** (Document T-05, page 71) are provided for handling the CPE credits that instructors may earn.
- Similarly, an **Author/Developer CPE Submittal Form** (Document T-06, page 72) and an **Author/Developer CPE Certificate Template** (Document T-07 page 73) are provided for handling the CPE credits that the program developers may earn.

The last two items include a final **Confirmation of Compliance Checklist** (Document T-08, page 74) and a list of **Program Closedown Procedures** (Document T-09, page 77).

That completes the inventory of the **CPE Field Guide**. Have at it, and good luck!

Define

The following cards are shown, layered:

- Measures of Success
- ROI
- Training Budget
- Business Goals
- Learning Objectives
- Delivery Methods

To do things differently,
we need to see things differently.

— Paul Allaire *(Xerox Chairman, Retired)*

Directions: Use the questions shown here to help you identify, analyze, understand, and validate the perceived need in order to make learning solution recommendations.

A. <u>Identify and understand the perceived need.</u>

1. **What is the business issue – how does what the client has differ from what the client wants?**
   - What is the gap between current and desired performance?

2. **What is driving this business issue?**
   - Have you received a specific request?
   - Has there been a strategic directive from leadership? (What group articulated the need?)
   - Have new competencies been identified?
   - Have we observed a measurable decline in performance, productivity, or profitability?
   - Has a new or reengineered system or process been introduced?
   - Have market conditions changed?

3. **What do we see as the benefits of meeting this need – for example, streamlined procedures, reduced costs, higher profitability, better employee retention?**
   - Besides these primary benefits, are there other, incidental benefits?

4. **What is the priority of this need compared to other business needs?**
   - When must this need be met?
   - Are there any special circumstances related to this need?

5. **Does the client have an idea on how to meet this need?**
   - What does this idea look like?
   - Is there consensus among other stakeholders about this idea?

6. **What do stakeholders expect from us – a recommendation, technical expertise, or a specific product or service?**
   - What does this idea look like?
   - Is there consensus among other stakeholders about this idea?

B. <u>Validate the need.</u>

1. **What "non-training" factors related to process, organization, and culture are contributing to this need?**
   - How much of this need is "trainable" – that is, will training actually solve the problem?

2. **What is the "life expectancy" of the target knowledge and skills – that is, are these competencies their people need for the long term?**

3. **How are these competencies currently being trained or learned?**
   - How have their people reacted to this approach?
   - What is it about the current approach that is not working?

4. **Has this or a similar project been undertaken before? By whom? What was the result?**
   - Has this specific problem been considered before? If so, what were the recommended solutions and their result?

———————— CONTINUED ———————— **Define T-01**

5. **What are the risks in trying to meet this need?**
   - Are sufficient resources – people, time, and money – available to see this effort through?
   - How quickly can decisions be made and sign-off obtained?
   - What are the risks of <u>not</u> meeting this need, of doing nothing?

C. <u>**Analyze a performance need in order to make recommendations**</u>.

1. **What are the job responsibilities or professional competencies related to this business need?**
   - Is there a priority among these tasks and competencies?
   - What does the client consider the minimum amount of learning time needed to address these competencies?
   - What is the maximum amount of learning time that can be reasonably dedicated, considering, for example, available budget, development and delivery resources, or participant time?

2. **Has similar training been developed or purchased – or is similar training under development?**
   - Who is responsible for its development and deployment?
   - How successful is/was this training?
   - Are materials from this training available for review and reuse?

3. **Who is the target audience?** (See **Audience Analysis** tool – **Define T-02**)
   - What about this audience would influence the type of solution proposed – for example, job level and function, location, age range and nationality?
   - What is their work environment like – job tasks, internal and external pressures, and so forth?
   - What are their incentives to attend and to learn? Do they have, or can they make, time to learn?
   - When is the right time for them to learn these competencies – that is, if we train them today will they be able to apply these competencies tomorrow?
   - Do they prefer traveling to central locations or learning in their own work environments?
   - Do they prefer self-study or group study – and is there a business need to "connect" either face-to-face or via technology with their colleagues.
   - What learning approaches have proven effective with this audience?
   - How much do they already know or how much can they already do in terms of this competency?
   - How frequently does the composition of this audience change?

4. **What are the learning environment resources and constraints?**
   - How would a proposed new learning solution, whether vendor-provided or internally developed, fit in with the current learning plan for members of this target audience?
   - What sort of training facilities, materials, equipment, and resources (including instructors) are commonly used or available?
   - How open to and supportive of various training media are the training delivery support personnel, information technology personnel, instructors, and other stakeholders?
   - What organizational constraints might affect the ability to implement a vendor product?

Define T-01

Directions: Before deciding to build or buy a learning program, ask questions to see whether some form of non-training solution makes better learning and business sense.

The BIG Question:
Are you sure there is a deficiency in professional competence (knowledge, skills, or abilities) that is causing the observed performance problem? Or might it be something else ... ?

1. **Performance support not training ...**

   Would some form of on-the-job support provide better results or a better return on investment than implementing a formal learning solution?

   - Would job aids or just-in-time tools and guidance make more sense?
   - Can members of the target audience be paired with or coached by more experienced people to learn from them?
   - Would new or different job challenges or assignments improve overall performance?

2. **Motivation and incentives ...**

   Is it that the audience does not know what to do or how to do it, or is it that they are <u>unwilling</u> to do it?

   - If they are unwilling, why do they lack the motivation?
     Do they disagree with a policy, is there a lack of support from leadership, or are there insufficient resources?

3. **Competition ...**

   Are there competing responsibilities – tasks that occupy the audience's time and attention – that prevent them from meeting performance expectations?

4. **Expectations, goals, performance measures ...**

   Do members of the audience have a clear understanding of what they are supposed to do and how their performance will be measured?

   - Do they receive adequate feedback so that they know where they are not performing up to expectations?

5. **Recruiting or staffing ...**

   Are these the right people for this task or responsibility?

   - Is the organization hiring or staffing the right people to perform these responsibilities?
   - Do the people in this position have the right background and personal attributes to succeed?

6. **Work environment ...**

   Are work conditions, procedures, or processes causing the problem?

   - Is the audience required to follow a process that is cumbersome, ill defined, or just unhelpful?
     Could they produce good, consistent results faster without following this process?
   - Is the physical environment – facilities, location, proximity, grouping, technology – conducive to meeting performance expectations?
   - Does the audience have access to the people and resources they need to make good decisions and fulfill their position responsibilities?

Define T-02

Directions: Use the questions listed here to help identify target audience characteristics that will affect the type of learning solution you recommend and the way that solution is designed.

1. **What are personnel classifications of your target audience (and related identifying information)?**
   - What is the range of job levels in your audience? What is the most common job level?
   - What is their job function or specialization?
   - What is the range and average tenure with the company?

2. **What is their work experience relevant to the learning or performance need?**
   - What is their knowledge of or background in the target knowledge and skills (competencies)?
   - How much relevant on-the-job experience do they have? In what sort of contexts have they gained this experience – for example, have they performed these skills only in high-priority, for-client projects?
   - How frequently do they use the target competencies and how critical are these competencies to their job responsibilities?

3. **What is their relevant training experience and their general attitude towards training?**
   - Have they had previous training in these competencies (and, if so, how effective or rewarding was that experience)?
   - What types of learning strategies and activities have been effective with this target audience?
   - What is their general attitude towards training? What are their incentives to attend training?

4. **What is their work environment like?**
   - What is their work environment like – tasks, internal/external pressures, physical arrangement?
   - Is their work team-based and project-focused or do they work individually and on long assignments?
   - Do they have time available to complete training – either by attending training out of the office or by completing a locally delivered program?
   - Do they have uninterrupted time available and access to equipment and other resources for pre-work and follow-on training?
   - What learning and performance support resources – for example, equipment, databases, mentors and coaches – are available in their workplace?

5. **What individual differences, preferences, and needs should you consider?**
   - How do they prefer to learn – e.g., in instructor-led group study or through self-study?
   - Do they prefer to travel to central locations to network or to stay in their own offices?
   - Are they interested in concepts, or do they want only practical, hands-on learning?
   - What should we avoid – that is, what is sure to discourage them or make them "tune out"?
   - Is English their native language? If not, how proficient are they in spoken English?

6. **What organizational factors affect them individually or as a group?**
   - How frequently does the audience change – is there a lot of turnover or job changing?
   - How is their performance measured – for example, revenue generated, customer service ratings, and/or internal review? How does attending training fit in with performance measures?
   - Have their job responsibilities changed recently (or will they change soon)?
   - Are they required to attend training for CPE credit or other professional requirements?

Define T-03

Directions: After setting your selection criteria, use this tool to: 1) compare delivery capabilities and constraints of common instructional delivery strategies, and 2) choose the strategy that fits your situation. (Note: Not all of these methods qualify for CPE.)

Strategy	Audience	Content	Learning Environment
Audiovisual Aids – any instructional media in audio or video form	▪ Geographically dispersed audience	▪ Knowledge and concepts ▪ Situations, skill demonstrations that must be seen	▪ Production costs and talent required (if new development) or can be a recording of a key message
Independent Study – educational process designed to permit a participant to learn a given subject under a learning contract with a CPE program sponsor	▪ Individual working with sponsor	▪ Specific to responsibility of position	▪ Make time in everyday activities ▪ Subject to specific NASBA guidelines
Instructor-Led (Group-Live) – classroom training in which instructors teach the subject matter to participants who are present in the classroom	▪ Networking and knowledge/ experience sharing ▪ Instructor can adapt to audience and event-specific needs ▪ Group- and team-based learning	▪ Convey common message to large groups ▪ Knowledge exchange – build on content – and feedback. ▪ Time-sensitive content ▪ Simulated tasks and practice opportunities.	▪ Central, regional, or local training sites. ▪ Need instructors qualified in the subject matter and the instructional methods ▪ May be supplemented with technology-based materials (blended strategy)
Job Aids – support materials or tools designed to help individuals during the actual performance of an on-the-job task	▪ Size varies ▪ Perform many routine tasks for which "Quick Reference" would help	▪ Reference content that addresses specific on-the-job tasks	▪ Can be paper- or computer-based ▪ Not for CPE credit
On-the-Job Learning – learning in the work environment doing work-required tasks. Can be based on action learning principles or coaching.	▪ Individual or team-based	▪ Skill-building via learn by doing in real-life setting ▪ Follow-up to formal training	▪ Access to experts (coaches, mentors) needed ▪ Generally not for CPE credit

———— CONTINUED ———————— **Define T-04**

Strategy	Audience	Content	Learning Environment
Research Databases & Online Communities – databases and online communities that are searchable repositories of data, information, and knowledge	▪ Large groups can have access using standard desktop applications	▪ Quick access to information ▪ Time-sensitive can be included if updated ▪ Large amounts of supplemental content	▪ Requires knowledge management to ensure quality of information ▪ Generally not for CPE credit
Self-Study (Interactive) – learning activity designed to permit a participant to learn the subject matter via a computer or other interactive device	▪ Usually learner controlled (how much adapts to learner depends on complexity of interactivity) ▪ Collaboration (depends on type of application)	▪ Programmed feedback (some use personal feedback through email) ▪ Consistent delivery ▪ Learner-to-subject matter Interaction	▪ Reduce travel costs ▪ High initial cost for new development/ purchase ▪ Technology resources and support required ▪ Must meet the applicable standards to qualify for CPE
Self-Study (Self-Paced) – self-paced instructional materials used in individual learning without major involvement of an instructor	▪ Learner-controlled, completed when and where needed	▪ Minimal feedback ▪ Present prerequisite knowledge for other learning events ▪ Consistent delivery of content that is not time-sensitive	▪ Reduce travel costs ▪ Portability of materials ▪ Generally not for CPE credit
Seminar – subject matter experts present information to large groups of people in one location. Can be done through videoconferencing to link experts with remote learners.	▪ Large groups in one location (or in several locations through teleconferencing) ▪ Networking ▪ Audience can hear speakers from outside the company	▪ Individual feedback may be limited ▪ Consistent information from experts ▪ "Gain awareness" ▪ Time-sensitive content	▪ Central, regional, or local facilities or technology to accommodate one-to-many delivery ▪ For CPE credit if part of instructional portion of a meeting

Strategy	Audience	Content	Learning Environment
Virtual Classroom – technology that provides live, interactive, web-based events for communicating with geographically dispersed participants	▪ Large group that is geographically dispersed ▪ Comfortable with distributed (not-in-person) group learning	▪ Consistent content to large groups delivered by expert ▪ Simulated tasks ▪ Helpful if content is in central repository	▪ Requires specific technology – Internet connection, software, headsets, etc. ▪ Can be delivered quickly, closer to time of need ▪ Reduce travel costs
Webcasting (Group Internet-Based) – an event broadcast over an intranet system so that all viewers receive the content at the same time, includes audio, can include video	▪ Large audience with needed intranet access and software ▪ No collaboration and learning is presented one-way to participants	▪ Keynote (motivational) messages featuring noted experts ▪ Time sensitive requiring quick distribution	▪ Infrastructure must be in place and technology support available ▪ Reduce travel costs ▪ Effective speaker needed ▪ Must meet the applicable standards to qualify for CPE
Workshop – a hands-on, participative session for small groups of participants	▪ Small groups ▪ Participative and hands-on ▪ Networking and collaboration ▪ Prior knowledge helpful	▪ Skill building ▪ Knowledge exchange – build on content – and feedback. ▪ Time-sensitive content	▪ Need equipment or simulated equipment for hands-on practice ▪ Often requires in-person learning

Define T-04

Directions: Use the questions in this tool to help you search for existing learning resources to use or reuse in meeting an identified learning need.

1. **Define what you are looking for.**
   - What is the learning need – what topic or competency area is involved?
   - What are the general goals? (You do not need specific objectives, but you should have a sense of the learning outcome you are hoping to achieve.)
   - Who is the audience for this learning need?

2. **Check internal knowledge repositories and contact others in your learning network.**
   - Do any existing professional development resources address this topic?
   - Are there any existing resources that address similar needs?

3. **Similarly check external sources via an internet search.**
   - Do any existing professional development resources address this topic?
   - Are there any existing resources that address similar needs?

4. **Qualify what you find to see if you can use it.**
   - Is it current, accurate, and appropriate to your audience?
   - What sort of modification needs to be done – updating, adding or deleting content, general editing, reorganizing, formatting, converting or migrating to a different delivery medium?
   - Do you estimate the total amount of modification needed to be within your time and budget constraints?

Define T-05

Directions: If you are looking to buy rather than build a learning program, use this checklist to help you evaluate vendors and their products. You should be able to answer **Yes** to every question. The "yes or no" questions are designed just to frame your discussion and introduce key topics with a vendor representative. Suggested follow-up questions are provided to help you qualify the vendor's answer.

Does the vendor course meet CPE requirements and does participation in this course qualify for CPE credit? ☐ Yes ☐ No
- Are the vendor courses NASBA certified?
- How many CPE credits does the learning program grant?

Does this vendor have a good reputation providing learning programs to our organization or other professional services organizations? ☐ Yes ☐ No
- What are some of these organizations?
- Have any of these organizations implemented this same learning program?

Has this vendor been in business long enough – and is their outlook bright enough – to make you confident that they will be in business for the long term? ☐ Yes ☐ No
- How large and stable is the vendor's client base?
- In what significant ways has the vendor grown over the last 3-5 years?

Are the vendor's products designed for an audience like your audience? ☐ Yes ☐ No
- How does the vendor ensure that the content, examples, and scenarios are realistic and relevant to an audience like yours?

Does the vendor put all learning products through careful review and quality assurance controls, including testing for usability and learning gain? ☐ Yes ☐ No
- Do they offer any sort of guarantee or warranty on their learning programs?

Has the vendor collected data on who uses its courses, "learner satisfaction" with the course, and impact on the customer's business? ☐ Yes ☐ No
- How does the vendor verify that their products have a positive impact on their clients' business?

Can the learning program be easily updated from either a content, instructional method, or delivery approach perspective? ☐ Yes ☐ No
- What are the typical costs for these sorts of updates?

Does the vendor provide technical support or train-the-trainer sessions if necessary? ☐ Yes ☐ No
- Are there additional costs?

Are the total costs for implementing this vendor's learning program comparable to those of other vendors? ☐ Yes ☐ No
- Are there any hidden costs associated with implementing the learning program?

Will the vendor provide demos or sample learning programs for you to review before making a decision? ☐ Yes ☐ No

---

Define T-06

Design

Creating something exceptional is not a matter of chance.
It is a matter of choice.

— Jim Collins *(Built to Last)*

Directions: Use this checklist to help you manage the development and delivery of a learning program. The checklist assumes that the program has already been defined, scoped, and approved in principle. **Note**: These guidelines may not be relevant to every situation. Also, the suggested timetables are ideals. In reality, timelines are typically much shorter.

TWO+ MONTHS prior to program

Instructional Content

- ❑ Identify design & development team. (Design T-02)
- ❑ Conduct the design meeting. (Design T-03)
- ❑ Develop the content outline. (Design T-05)
- ❑ Create learning objectives. (Design T-06, T-07)
- ❑ Determine learning methods and activities. (Design T-08)
- ❑ Prepare course description. (Design T-10)
- ❑ Determine program prerequisites, prior experience, and/or advanced prep requirements.
- ❑ Complete Master Design Document. (Design T-11)
- ❑ Obtain all necessary approvals of design.
- ❑ Assemble development team, document credentials. (Develop T-01)
- ❑ Develop program content. (Develop T-02 – T-07)
- ❑ Complete quality assurance assessment. (Develop T-08)
- ❑ Document developer review. (Develop T-09)
- ❑ Document independent technical review. (Develop T-10)
- ❑ Pilot test program as appropriate. (Develop T-11)
- ❑ Complete final instructional materials.
- ❑ Determine final CPE credits by field of study. (Develop T-12)

Administration & Logistics

- ❑ Identify training dates.
- ❑ Determine level / number of participants to attend.
- ❑ Establish detailed budget.
- ❑ Reserve facility (meeting and sleeping rooms, as needed) and arrange for supporting technology.
- ❑ Set up registration tracking procedure.
- ❑ Identify qualified instructors, document credentials. (Deliver T-01)
- ❑ Announce program – including dates, times, and location – to target audience. Include all CPE required information: session title & description, learning objectives, program level, delivery methods, prerequisites & advanced prep, CPE credits (by field of study), and registration and other related procedures.

CONTINUED ——————— **Design T-01**

ONE MONTH prior to program

Instructional Content
- ❏ Distribute instructional materials to instructors.
- ❏ Hold instructor preparation session(s).

Administration & Logistics
- ❏ Review registration count and follow up with those who have not registered.
- ❏ Send logistics information to instructors – dates, times, training location, travel and housing arrangements, and instructions regarding expenses.
- ❏ Organize participant arrival and departure times and make specific housing arrangements as necessary for instructors and participants.

TWO WEEKS prior to program

Administration & Logistics
- ❏ Complete inventory of all training materials required for conduct.
- ❏ Send registration confirmation to participants, including information about housing, training location, and directions or maps.
- ❏ Distribute/post pre-work and other program materials as appropriate.
- ❏ Verify instructor arrival and departure times and make sure they have received their materials.
- ❏ Arrange transportation for participants and instructors.
- ❏ Ensure that all session materials are shipped and received.

ON (OR BEFORE) DAY of program

Instructional Content
- ❏ Hold instructor meeting for final preparation. (Prep guidance in Deliver T02 – T-06)

Administration & Logistics
- ❏ Finalize the list of participants, including name and office location.
- ❏ Prepare sign-in sheet for CPE records. (Deliver T-07)
- ❏ Monitor transportation and housing arrangements.
- ❏ Ensure that meeting spaces are set up correctly.

CONTINUED —————— **Design T-01**

DURING program

<u>Instructional Content</u>
- ❑ Support unanticipated instructional needs as they arise.

<u>Administration & Logistics</u>
- ❑ Manage sign-in sheet to monitor attendance, noting those who arrive late and/or leave early.
- ❑ Provide evaluation forms to participants. (Document T-01)
- ❑ Provide evaluation forms to instructors. (Document T-02)

AFTER the program

<u>Instructional Content</u>
- ❑ Compile and summarize evaluation data, share with development and instructor team.
- ❑ Conduct debrief session with developers and instructors, and document revisions to be made in the future.
- ❑ Identify content refresh schedule.

<u>Administration & Logistics</u>
- ❑ Issue participant CPE certificates as appropriate. (Document T-03)
- ❑ Secure instructor CPE information and issue instructor CPE certificates as appropriate. (Document T-04, T-05)
- ❑ Secure author/developer CPE information and issue author/developer certificates as appropriate. (Document T-06, T-07)
- ❑ Prepare budget-to-actual comparison, complete financial assessment.
- ❑ Confirm compliance with CPE standards. (Document T-08)
- ❑ Prepare CPE documentation closedown file. (see Document T-09 for detail)

Design T-01

Directions: This document articulates the business case for developing a particular CPE program and ensures thorough upfront planning.

PROGRAM	
Working Title	
Short Description	
High-Level Objective(s) and Desired Outcomes	
Target Delivery / Release Date	
BUSINESS CASE	
Business Driver(s) and Organizational Benefits	
Connection to Other Initiatives	
Direct Costs	
Financial Benefits	
AUDIENCE	
Primary Audience	
Audience Attributes (size, geography, demographics)	
Prior Knowledge / Experience Expected	
PROGRAM ATTRIBUTES	
Delivery Mode / Media	
Program Length	
Estimated CPE by Field of Study	
Content Shelf-Life	
Key Learning Resources to be Created	

——————— CONTINUED ——————— **Design T-02**

St. Charles
Consulting Group
© 2010

DELIVERY REQUIREMENTS	
Facility / Technology Implications	
Instructor / Facilitator Requirements	
PROJECT PLAN	
Implementation Plan	
Evaluation Plan	
PROJECT TEAM	
Sponsor	
Project Manager	
Subject Matter Expert(s)	
Instructional Designer(s)	
Independent Technical Reviewer(s)	
Other Key Players	

Design T-02

Directions: Use this tool to plan a design meeting in which you will collaboratively build the content outline for a new or revised learning program.

Meeting Logistics / Time and Place
- 4 hours suggested; large enough room to spread out and post flipcharts.

Participants
- Ensure that the following perspectives are represented: the sponsor, subject matter experts (SMEs), people who clearly understand the target audience and the work that they do, and instructional design expertise.

Purpose and Outcomes
To begin the design of [LEARNING SOLUTION]. Expected outcomes include:
- Content outline that highlights key learning points
- Some ideas for delivering each content piece (as time allows)

Preparatory Reading
- Learning need/project background notes [ATTACH]
- Audience analysis table – characteristics and design implications [ATTACH]

Time	Lead	Topic
8:00 – 8:15		**Welcome: Who's who and what we need to have done by meeting's end** • Introductions • Purpose, outcomes, agenda, ground rules
8:15 – 8:30		**Warm-up: The good and the bad in training** • Think of a great training or learning experience you have had. Then think of a not-so-great experience. What made the difference? (Capture and post.)
8:30 – 9:15		**Review and discussion of design meeting pre-read** • What project history should we know before talking about the design? • What do we need to keep in mind about this audience? • What do we need to keep in mind about this learning need?
9:15 – 11:00 (10-min. break included)		**Building the content outline** 1. Brainstorm learning task related to course subject matter. 2. Group learning tasks. 3. Sequence learning tasks (if appropriate). 4. Review content outline: – Eliminate nonessential content. – Make sure key points are highlighted and reinforced. – Check overall coherence of content structure.
11:00 – 11:45		**Quick brainstorm of design ideas** • Pre-session ideas – strategies for preparing participants to make the most of the session • During session ideas – Ideas for learning strategies and activities for 3 most important content topics • Post-session ideas – strategies for follow-on learning
11:45 – 12:00		**Wrap-up and next steps** • Use content outline to write goals and learning objectives (instructional designer) and send to SME for review.

Design T-03

© 2010

Directions: NASBA standards require that "learning programs must be developed by individuals or teams having expertise in the subject matter." Subject matter experts (or SMEs) make sure your content is technically accurate and current. They also ensure that learning activities are appropriate for a given audience and for the stated learning goals. Use the following guidelines to ensure that you make the best use of your SME's time and expertise.

1. **Allocate content expertise by time, not by head.**
   - You need a SME, which means, you need a SME's <u>time</u>. Make sure your SME has the availability to provide and review content within your project timelines.

2. **Look for content and <u>context</u> expertise.**
   - Try to find a SME who is both a content expert and a <u>context</u> expert – that is, one who knows from first-hand experience about the day-to-day, on-the-job life of your target audience. The benefits to your design will be considerable.

3. **Set clear expectations.**
   - Make sure your SME knows up front what is expected in terms of providing accurate, up-to-date content and reviewing design documents and developed materials. Again, make sure your SME has the time to be an active participant.

4. **Prepare for managing information and content overload.**
   - Subject matter experts often see all aspects of the job or task or content as equally important. They may be right, but your course must focus on the most important, most relevant, most immediately useful information (the "need to know" rather than the "nice to know").

5. **Involve your SME in the design.**
   - Design of the learning program is not solely your prerogative. Let your subject matter experts become partners in design.

6. **Give your SME something to react to.**
   - Since it is easier (and faster) to critique than to create, give your SME things to react to – documented ideas, design details, developed materials. Encourage candid critique of everything you present to a SME.

7. **Make sure a technical reviewer signs off on the material.**
   - Once a program is substantially designed and developed, the material must be reviewed for accuracy, currency, and sufficiency by one or more qualified persons other than those who developed it.

Design T-04

Directions: Follow these step-by-step guidelines to build a content outline collaboratively with your subject matter expert. Prepare by reviewing your analysis data on the learning need and the target audience.

1. Brainstorm topics and tasks.

- On a flipchart or whiteboard, write this guiding question: "What does our audience need to know or be able to do to bridge the gap between current performance and desired performance?"
- Brainstorm topics or tasks to be learned.
- Give each person a stack of large sticky notes.
- Give individuals 10 minutes or so to write down (silently) a single topic or task on each note.

2. Group or cluster topics or tasks to be learned.

- Post sticky notes one by one on a wall or whiteboard, grouping tasks together by affinity, priority, or interaction type.
- Continue brainstorming as a group and posting responses in the appropriate groups.
- Check that you have captured all need-to-know tasks by asking, "What else do participants need to know or be able to do in this regard?"
- When you have exhausted the topic, look for clusters that can be combined.
- Create a label for each essential-to-the-job task cluster using additional sticky notes.

3. Sequence clusters of topics or tasks.

Take the essential task labels and arrange them in an order that makes sense given this overall learning need. Here are some ways to sequence:

- "Big picture" to details (or vice versa)
- Step-by-step chronology
- Simple to complex by learning type (knowledge, understanding, application, analysis, etc.)

4. Review content outline.

- Use the categorizing scheme – 1) essential to the job, 2) relevant and useful, or 3) interesting and potentially relevant – to make sure you have identified truly essential topics or tasks.
- Continue your review using these questions:
  - Does the content as outlined fully address each key learning point?
  - Do topics build on each other and reinforce each piece of prior learning?
  - Have all nonessential tasks been removed?
  - Does the sequence present a good distribution of the more active, intrinsically motivating topics with those that may be less intrinsically engaging?
  - Do the first and last topics make a powerful first impression and an equally (or more) powerful last impression?

5. Identify learning program goals.

- Take the label you gave each topic or task cluster and rewrite it (if and as needed) to be one of the three to five overall learning goals for your learning program. Identifying the overall learning goals will help prepare you for your next design step: Writing learning objectives.

Design T-05

St. Charles
Consulting Group

© 2010

Directions: The program developer should use this guide – while looking over the content outline for the proposed course – to define learning objectives and program goals.

1. **Start with the audience and an introductory phrase.**
   - Bring to mind again the audience for whom you are designing.
   - Work that audience into a phrase to introduce your program's learning objectives. For example: "Upon completion of this course (or module), participants will be able to …"

2. **Look over each topic or learning task grouping in the content outline.**
   - For each topic or learning task grouping, try to capture in a single phrase the key knowledge, skills, and/or abilities that participants must demonstrate.

3. **Check the verb used in each phrase to make sure that it is specific and measurable behavior.**
   Here are some sample verbs:
   - For <u>knowledge</u>: name, list, label, state, define, describe, recognize, recall, relate
   - For <u>comprehension</u>: compare, contrast, identify, classify, explain, illustrate
   - For <u>applying knowledge</u>: perform, demonstrate, use, apply, interpret
   - For <u>analysis or synthesis of concepts</u>: diagram, categorize, differentiate, design, create, compose
   - For <u>evaluation and making judgments</u>: choose, challenge, reject, evaluate, judge, value, predict

4. **Review each objective to make sure it is an outcome.**
   - Make sure you have created learning objectives, not learning activity descriptions or agenda items. In other words, make sure each objective describes what participants will be able to know or do <u>as a result</u> of the learning activity.

5. **Define the context in which each behavior is demonstrated.**
   - What is the context (condition) in which this audience should demonstrate this behavior? In other words, in what situation and using what tools should participants demonstrate the knowledge, skill, or ability captured in each behavior?

6. **Identify program goals.**
   - Identify program goals (so-called "terminal objectives") – those top-level objectives that represent culminating behaviors. For example, if the entire learning program addresses a new process to follow, the terminal objectives are related to the major steps in that process. "Enabling objectives" are substeps that lead to each terminal objective.

7. **Document learning objectives and begin to document learning activity ideas.**
   - Document the learning objectives in the appropriate sequence (to fit your content outline) and send them to your SME for review.
   - Look again at the behavior and context in which that behavior is performed and write down any ideas for learning activities that will help participants achieve those objectives.

Design T-06

Directions: Creating a table like the one below, develop a comprehensive "ABC" learning objective using the following steps:

1. In the top section, briefly define the target audience.
2. List the desired behaviors using the suggested verbs.
3. Identify the context for behavior for each desired behavior listed.
4. Combine this information to write a comprehensive learning objective.

Target Audience:

Desired Behavior	Context for Behavior	Learning Objective

Design T-07

Directions: After choosing general instructional methods, use this tool to decide what learning activities you should use to help participants achieve each learning objective.

Activity	Design and Development Notes	Delivery Notes
Case study A thinly disguised business problem that requires participants to analyze data, define issues, and generate solutions	▪ Takes time, subject matter expertise, and good short-story writing skills to develop a good case (case studies can also be purchased) ▪ Developer will need to outline several possible solutions to each problem in the case ▪ Often requires advance preparation (reading the case and related data) ▪ Can frustrate participants if insufficient information is provided ▪ Usually requires participants to do some additional research and data gathering online	▪ Takes time to deliver (a few hours to a few days), but logistics vary with complexity of the case ▪ Instructor should be a skilled facilitator of discussion who also has good knowledge of the case ▪ Maximize collaboration and consider building in some friendly competition
Discussion Moderated, facilitated, or participant-led discussions can take several forms: small group, large group, or expert panel	▪ Fairly easy to develop – participants supply most of the content – but thought should be given to developing stimulating discussion topics and questions ▪ Difficult to control the quality of information being shared (depends on participant knowledge of subject matter) ▪ Good for participant involvement and knowledge sharing ▪ Can often be used as a follow-up to a skill building activity	▪ Takes up more time than lecture, but can lead to deeper understanding ▪ Instructor should have good facilitation skills to keep discussions focused and moving. ▪ For good panel discussions need to have experts present who are prepared to talk about the topic
Drill and practice Rapid, repeated questions and exercises to reinforce newly learned information and skills	▪ Very good for learning facts and building skills but since it has a "schoolhouse feel" adults may dislike this approach ▪ Use an iterative process, such as: 1) do the skill (respond), 2) receive feedback, 3) repeat the skill (respond)	▪ Instructor needs to be an effective coach who can push participants and make it rigorous and challenging without discouraging or boring participants
Energizer Short, engaging activity designed to help participants refocus their energy on learning	▪ Get participants up and moving, but keep it short, no more than 5 minutes ▪ Have a few energizers on hand to use as needed (not formally scheduled)	▪ Often used in between long periods of inactivity at the instructor's discretion ▪ May distract too much – the fun of the energizer makes the course content that much less exciting

———————————————— CONTINUED ————————— **Design T-08**

Activity	Design and Development Notes	Delivery Notes
Game Opportunity to practice knowledge and skills in a motivational context in which there are set rules and a clear goal	<ul><li>Because they are competitive, games are highly motivating to some but discouraging to others</li><li>Often reuses an existing game format with which participants are familiar (otherwise can be time consuming to develop, explain, and deliver)</li><li>Require clear rules that are impartial and easy to understand or participants can get frustrated</li><li>Better as a team-based activity</li><li>Generally used to reinforce information already presented rather than to present new information</li></ul>	<ul><li>Can be used as needed as part energizer, part drill and practice</li><li>Instructor needs to keep competition friendly and respectful</li><li>"If they are having fun, they must be learning" is an oversimplification</li><li>A better guiding principle would be, "If they are mentally engaged, they are learning"</li></ul>
Goal-based scenario (GBS) A simulation in which participants work within set parameters towards achieving the goal(s) defined by their scenario	<ul><li>Complex activity that requires time to design and experience</li><li>Usually addresses multiple objectives</li><li>Need to design a specific mission that takes place in a simulated but workplace-relevant environment</li></ul>	<ul><li>Takes time to deliver – one day to one week</li><li>Often requires instructors and outside visitors to play roles</li></ul>
Guided reflection Activity in which participants reconstruct an experience with a "moral" – that is, lessons learned from the experience	<ul><li>Used as a way to debrief a learning activity or to turn an on-the-job experience into a learning activity</li><li>Instructor/facilitator can use several formats, for example:</li><li>– 1) What happened? 2) What are the lessons learned from this experience? 3) How will you use these lessons learned in similar situations? 4) What specific "similar situations" are coming up?</li><li>– 1) What happened? 2) How is what happened like what you expected? 3) How is it different from what you expected?</li></ul>	<ul><li>Can be delivered as separate activity or as a debrief to any learning activity</li><li>Instructor should have good facilitation skills</li></ul>

Activity	Design and Development Notes	Delivery Notes
Icebreaker Icebreakers help participants get to know each other and are meant to establish and promote a cooperative and collegial learning environment	▪ Used at the start of group-based learning to help instructors and participants get to know each other ▪ Often asks participants to pair up, answer some specific information (name, office, function, something more personal or relevant to the course topic), and then introduce each other	▪ Needs to be well facilitated so does not take up more time than it should ▪ Participants should be prompted to "do a professional job" of introducing one another
Imaging Activity whereby participants communicate their thoughts and attitudes by creating graphical representations	▪ Some audiences really enjoy this, others do not ▪ Participants who think they lack artistic talents may find the task intimidating; they may prefer to work cooperatively (in groups) ▪ Can be used to prompt participants to visualize a concept, or their view of a concept ▪ Can also be used to review information	▪ Participants can use own piece of paper, but often works better using large, flipchart paper ▪ Takes time to do and review – participants generally like to share their drawings
Journaling Participants reflect on some topic, question, or events and record their reflections in writing	▪ Often used as a "brain writing" exercise in which participants write for a set period of time (5 minutes) on a set topic without taking the pen off the paper ▪ Should have a time or page limit ▪ Topic or question on which participants write should be specific, meaningful, and engaging (stimulating ideas) ▪ Can be used as a motivational activity to find out what prior knowledge participants have about the topic	▪ Can be done in class (keep it short) or between sessions of a longer training event. Often have better results in class. ▪ Can be used as a debrief activity in which participants document what they will do with the new knowledge and skills when they return to their offices

Activity	Design and Development Notes	Delivery Notes
Lecture/presentation Instructors/presenters who are content experts present information in their own words, often using supplemental media (flipcharts, presentation slides) and soliciting questions from the audience	▪ Dissemination of information relies on instructors/presenters who are content experts ▪ Supplemental media (flipcharts, presentation slides) enhance the presentation ▪ Good questions, especially good follow up questions, can make the presentation more engaging ▪ Takes less time to design and develop than other instructional methods ▪ Inexperienced instructors require more support (instructor materials have to be more robust)	▪ Generally takes less time to deliver knowledge and information ▪ Short 15-minute presentations often precede skill practice activities ▪ Presenter should be an engaging, facilitative instructor ▪ Too many presentation slides deter from the presentation – every slide must matter
Models and maps Simplified, graphical representations of concepts, procedures, or processes	▪ Simple, concrete models can be more helpful to many learners ▪ Models help participants understand concepts and how concepts relate to each other; can make information easier to grasp, especially in the "big picture" ▪ Often require expertise in layout and graphics; could subject to brand standards for visuals	▪ Can be created and displayed ahead of time ▪ If it is necessary to show flow or movement, consider creating the model or map on a flipchart while participants watch ▪ Usually presented in presentation slides or in handouts
Problem solving An intellectual skill activity that requires individuals to apply rules and principles in given situations	▪ Works best for learning that can be defined as a step-by-step process; may not fit learning outcomes that have no specific or known solution, such as how to coach a specific individual in a specific place at a specific time ▪ Takes time and expertise to create challenging, context-specific problems ▪ Solution steps often depicted as flowchart or decision tree	▪ Instructor often goes through the process and a sample problem first ▪ Often more effective (more skills learned) as group process ▪ Debrief is key element; participants must be asked to "show their work" by explaining their reasoning

St. Charles
Consulting Group
© 2010

Activity	Design and Development Notes	Delivery Notes
Reading comprehension Participants read an informational piece, answer comprehension questions or make inferences and evaluations	▪ Can be designed as a small group or large group discussion ▪ Reading material should be relevant to knowledge and skills to be learned ▪ Instructor guide needs specific questions to check comprehension	▪ Reading passages can be handed out in paper or placed online in a course database
Role-Play Dramatic simulations in which participants assume specific roles and are asked to behave as that role and situation demand	▪ Drawback is that effectiveness depends on the energy and experience that an individual puts into playing the role ▪ May be more effective to create a dramatic situation (a scenario) and ask participants to be themselves ▪ Can design a specific scenario or just the general framework of a scenario (e.g., a time when you worked with a challenging teammate) and ask participants to provide their own details ▪ Very appropriate to interpersonal skills learning and addressing attitudes underlying certain behavior	▪ Much less threatening to have participants perform a role-play in small groups rather than in front of the entire class ▪ Role-plays can address knowledge and skills, but they are also particularly suited to addressing attitudes – the "why" underneath the knowledge and skill learning ▪ If a complex role is needed, have an instructor or "special guest" play that part ▪ Provide the player with talking points to prepare from rather than full scripts
Self-Assessment A formal or informal instrument or activity that a participant uses individually to gauge his or her own knowledge or skill level	▪ Can create a self-assessment for a specific topic or purchase an existing instrument if it fits with the course goals ▪ Can be paper-based or online ▪ If used as pre-work, have to have a way of ensuring that participants will actually do it ▪ Participants often score themselves	▪ Often used as pre-work or early in a training course to help participants set their own learning goals and identify areas of strength and areas to develop

——————— CONTINUED ——————— **Design T-08**

Activity	Design and Development Notes	Delivery Notes
Simulations and scenarios Simulations create representations of real situations so that participants can apply their knowledge and practice their skills in a safe but realistic environment	▪ Takes time to prepare a realistic, content-rich simulation ▪ Have to provide some challenge in the simulation; opportunities to make mistakes and learn from those mistakes ▪ Can create scenarios and situations in which participants are themselves ▪ There is no single correct answer, although some solutions may be better than others. Sample solutions need to be prepared and included in feedback	▪ Participants must see the consequences of decisions they make ▪ Can be high-tech (computer based) or low-tech (classroom based with handouts)
Skill demonstration (Behavior modeling) Demonstrations allow participants to view a process in action or a procedure performed by an expert Instructors model the behaviors that participants are to develop as an effective instructional method	▪ Often used as the first step in teaching how to do a specific procedure ▪ Participants learn from observing others' behaviors and the consequences others experience as a result of their behavior ▪ Need expert to model the behavior either live or on video (digital or analog) – benefit to video is ability to pause, rewind, and replay as many times as participants need	▪ Can be delivered via video or live ▪ With instructor-led training (ILT), the instructor must be able to model the behaviors they are trying to teach (e.g., those teaching a presentations course should be strong presenters)
Socratic dialog (Socratic method) A teaching method whereby instructors or facilitators ask open-ended questions (and challenging follow-up questions) to encourage participants to create and critique their own learning	▪ In a Socratic dialog instructors do not provide the answers ▪ Requires high level of expertise and excellent questioning skills on the part of the instructor (materials should provide robust lists of questions) ▪ Can also be used to address a set learning topic or to simply to "plant a seed" in the learner's mind ▪ Better when used with general concepts to which there are no clear or easy answers	▪ Instructor/facilitator must be able to effectively and in a friendly manner prompt participants to find their own answers or challenge their own assumptions ▪ Should have the some of the rigor and feel of a drill to it

——————— CONTINUED ——————— **Design T-08**

© 2010   St. Charles
Consulting Group

Activity	Design and Development Notes	Delivery Notes
Storytelling Instructors or participants narrate experiences that illustrate or serve as an analogy of a key learning point	▪ Can demonstrate a principle in action through a dramatic telling of events ▪ Often referred to as "war stories" in which more seasoned instructors share their experiences with participants, highlighting lessons learned and how those lessons learned can be leveraged by participants	▪ Important ingredient is to prompt participants to think of their own "war stories"
Teach-back Participants "teach back" newly learned knowledge or skills to their fellow participants	▪ Good for covering multiple topics of information in a more engaging way ▪ Generally done in teams, participants given a specific topic to present (each group gets a different topic); they either use their own combined knowledge or do research (if sources available) and then present their findings to the class ▪ Self-critique, peer feedback, and instructor feedback should follow each teach-back	▪ Instructors should prompt teams to do a professional presentation – for example, present findings as if presenting to a client team or a proposal review committee ▪ Provide time for participants to prepare and rehearse their presentation ▪ Use a timer and hold participants accountable for keeping their presentation within time limits
Video Participants and instructor watch video clips	▪ Good for showing examples and "non-examples" of specific behaviors ▪ Also good for showing a specific procedure because you can pause, rewind, etc. ▪ Original video is expensive to produce – requires scripts, camera crews, editing, etc. – more cost-effective to obtain existing video that addresses learning needs	▪ Important to have video set to appropriate spot and volume checked before instruction ▪ Videos should be presented in short segments (15 minutes maximum)

Design T-08

Directions: Use this tool to bring certain theoretical learning principles to life in your program.

Theory	Pertinent Points	Practical Application
Behaviorism	a. Learning is a change in observable behavior. b. Learning should be shaped by a series of reinforcements and intermittent reinforcement causes a longer lasting behavior change.	a. Focus your objectives on what participants would do to <u>show</u> they have learned. b. Provide ongoing but intermittent reinforcement for each step learned and inject some element of surprise or unpredictability to increase motivation.
Social Learning	a. People can improve competence by observing modeled behaviors and their consequences. b. Environment, personal characteristics, and behavior are interrelated.	a. Have a respected person demonstrate the desired behavior and attitude and make sure participants discuss and, whenever possible, experience the good and bad consequences of behaviors. b. In your design, give thought not just to the content but the environment in which participants will learn that content.
Cognitive Theory and Information Processing	a. There are different types of learning – stating facts, solving problems, making choices, performing acts, monitoring one's own learning. b. Tasks consist of subtasks that must be learned. c. People create mental frameworks based on their experiences. These frameworks help them generalize from a past experience to a new experience. d. Contrasts between concepts should be emphasized. e. Concepts need to be thoroughly learned ("consolidated") before new ones are introduced. f. Learning occurs through the active involvement of learners with their environment.	a. Choose a learning activity that fits the type of learning in each learning objective – for example, if the learning objective involves performing an act, choose a learning activity that allows each participant to perform the act and receive feedback on that performance. b. Break tasks to be learned into subtasks and use learning activities that address each subtask as well as the overall task; organize these subtasks (or "chunks" of learning) so that new learning builds on previous. c. Determine what participants already know and connect this prior knowledge to new learning; provide an "advance organizer," a visual framework to help participants organize what they are learning. d. Make sure participants encounter key concepts several times in several formats and highlight the contrasts in these key concepts. e. Provide sufficient practice in each concept before moving on to new concepts. f. Create a learning environment that encourages participation, stimulates informed guessing, and promotes problem solving.

——————— CONTINUED ——————————— **Design T-09**

St. Charles
Consulting Group
© 2010

Theory	Pertinent Points	Practical Application
Constructivist and Situated Learning Theory	a. Knowledge cannot be "objectified" and "transferred" to learners. Knowledge is subjective and is constructed individually by each learner. b. Learning is an active process in which learners construct new ideas or concepts based on their current and past knowledge. c. Learning should occur in contexts or situations that are similar to those in which this new learning will be used.	a. Immerse participants in an environment that is rich in information, real-world tasks, and discussion. Create a learning environment that mirrors the participants' work environment. b. Have instructors facilitate rather than directly instruct and use techniques such as a Socratic dialog to encourage and challenge participants to: 1) discover principles for themselves, 2) compare and contrast what they learn with what they already know, and 3) make sense out of new experiences or concepts. c. Create a training environment that looks and feels like the work environment.

Design T-09

Directions: Detailed course descriptions helps others assess the appropriateness of a professional development option, and they are necessary for CPE compliance. As you develop the program and prepare for delivery, include the following items in the course description that you use to promote the course.

1. **Program Title** – Select a title that quickly conveys what the program is about.

2. **Program Description** – Use your business plan document, content outline, and learning objectives as input for describing the major topics covered.

3. **Learning Objectives and Outcomes** – List the defined learning objectives and the behavioral outcomes that are expected.

4. **Intended Audience** – Describe the audience for whom the CPE program was developed.

5. **Program Level** – Identify the appropriate program level:
   - Basic – most beneficial to professionals new to a skill or attribute; often for individuals at the entry-level.
   - Intermediate – builds on a basic program and is most appropriate for those with detailed knowledge in an area; often for mid-level personnel with supervisory responsibilities.
   - Advanced – most useful for individuals with mastery of the particular topic; focuses on the development of in-depth knowledge, a variety of skills, or a broader range of applications; generally for "seasoned professionals" or those with specialized knowledge.
   - Update – provides a general review of new developments; for participants who need to keep current in a subject area.
   - Overview – provides a general review of the subject area from a broad perspective; appropriate for professionals at all levels.

6. **Instructional Delivery Methods** – Summarize the instructional methods used to meet learning objectives – for example, instructor-led group study, case studies, role-plays, simulations, Internet-based study, or self-study resources.

7. **Prerequisites** – Identify any prerequisite education or experience required to achieve the course objectives.

8. **Advance Preparation** – Indicate any preparatory assignment (pre-work, pre-read) that participants must complete before the session is held.

9. **Recommended CPE Credit (by Field of Study)** – Identify the number of CPE credits in each field of study involved in the program. NASBA Standards define one CPE credit as "fifty minutes of participation in a group, independent study or self-study program." A course that runs from 8 a.m. to 5 p.m. with one hour for lunch and two 15-minute breaks merits 9 CPE credit hours (540 total minutes - 90 minutes lunches/breaks = 450 qualifying minutes/50 = 9 CPE credits).

10. **Facility & Technology Requirements** – Describe any special requirements related to the physical environment for the training program.

11. **Course Registration Requirements** – Explain how potential participants can register for this course and what approval may be required. If payment by the learner is required, the sponsor's refund policy and complaint resolution policy should also be stated.

Design T-10

Directions: A master design document serves as the blueprint for guiding the CPE program development. It is also a very helpful document when describing the "big picture" for sponsors, instructors, and others. Chart the entire flow of the program by using a template such as the one provided here, starting with a high-level agenda and following with a description of each learning segment.

Program Agenda

Time	Topic / Activity	Presenter(s)
8:00 – 9:00 a.m.	Welcome & Program Overview	Tim Burnett
9:00 – 10:00 a.m.	International Tax	Scott Limbaugh
10:00 – 10:30 a.m.	BREAK	—
10:30 – 11:30 a.m.	Multi-State Tax	Adam Sonenstein
11:30 a.m. – 12:30 p.m.	Family Wealth Planning	Frankie Skinner
12:30 – 1:30 p.m.	LUNCH	—
2:30 – 3:30 p.m.	Corporate Tax	Larry Davenport
3:30 – 4:00 p.m.	BREAK	—
4:00 – 5:00 p.m.	Pass-Thru Entities	Gerry Lane-Morris
5:00 – 6:00 p.m.	Non-Profit Tax	Robin Newcombe
7:00 – 10:00 p.m.	GROUP DINNER	—
Total CPE: 8 in Taxes		

Detailed Design

Learning Segment	Min.	Purpose	Instructional Methods	Content Sources	Notes
Module 1 – Welcome and Program Overview – Tim Burnett					
Instructor introduction	5	Focus attention on topic	Fill-in-blank exercise	National statistics	Handout:Exercise Slide with statistics
Participant introductions	20	Getting to know one another	Self-introductions, describe first paying job		
Overview/ groundrules	35	Overview of program	Lecture and group discussion	Program Profile	Slides showing modular layout and descriptions
Module Time	60				
Module 2 – International Tax – Scott Limbaugh					
etc.					

Continue matrix as necessary to capture all learning segments.

Design T-11

Develop

Knowledge of how to combine
is the mother of all other forms of knowledge.

— Alexis de Tocqueville *(Democracy in America)*

Directions: Use this form to document to document the members of the program's development team, the independent technical reviewer, and their specific qualifications as subject matter experts in technical content or instructional design.

LEAD TECHNICAL DEVELOPER				
Name	**Program Contributions**	**Qualifications**	**CPA?**	
			Y	N

OTHER TECHNICAL DEVELOPER(S) & SUBJECT MATTER EXPERT(S)				
Name(s)	**Program Contributions**	**Qualifications**	**CPA?**	
			Y	N
			Y	N
			Y	N
			Y	N
			Y	N

INSTRUCTIONAL DESIGNER(S)				
Name(s)	**Program Contributions**	**Qualifications**	**CPA?**	
			Y	N
			Y	N
			Y	N
			Y	N
			Y	N

INDEPENDENT TECHNICAL REVIEWER(S)				
			Y	N
			Y	N

Develop T-01

Directions: Use this tool to help you decide what learning materials make the most sense for the learning program you are developing.

	Materials	Notes
☐	**Agenda**	▪ The instructor agenda lists topics and timings.
		▪ The participant version of the agenda does not list timings.
☐	**E-book (e-workbook)**	▪ An e-book is made up of electronic information presented as an organized book and distributed through e-mail or by posting on an accessible site.
		▪ An e-book may include features of digital text – searchable, links, attached files, and pop-up windows for additional information.
		▪ An e-book can be saved in several file formats, such as PDF or HTML files.
☐	**Evaluations (feedback forms)**	▪ Evaluations – both participant and instructor feedback forms – are helpful for all training events.
		▪ Surveys and questionnaires can also be used as evaluation instruments to measure the effectiveness of a learning solution.
☐	**Facilitator Guide (FG)**	▪ Like an instructor guide (IG), the facilitator guide is a step-by-step guide used to facilitate a training course.
		▪ FGs are used when the lead role is filled not by a SME but by a facilitator whose job is to facilitate discussions and activities, not to present any substantive content.
		▪ FG directions should focus on set up, conduct, and debriefing of activities.
☐	**Flipcharts**	▪ Many flipcharts can be created ahead of time, but flipcharts are also good for creating diagrams or illustrating concepts in the moment.
		▪ Flipcharts are excellent for recording and posting participant ideas, comments, and questions.
		▪ Instructors can use flipcharts to summarize activity directions to participants.
☐	**Handouts**	▪ Handouts are usually created for participants to support a learning activity.
		▪ If a course contains many handouts, they should be sequenced and stapled into a packet or assembled into a participant workbook.
		▪ Handouts should be numbered for easy reference by instructors and participants.
		▪ Handouts of "sample solutions" should be created for case studies and other activities and distributed to participants after the activity.
		▪ Often handouts are presented electronically – on a CD-ROM or flash drive – and participants are asked only to print as needed.
☐	**Instructor CD-ROM**	▪ If a learning program contains digital media such as presentation slides and audio clips, the media can be burned on a CD-ROM (especially if the learning program will be repeated).

CONTINUED ——————— **Develop T-02**

St. Charles
© 2010   Consulting Group

	Materials	Notes
☐	Instructor Guide (IG)	■ In instructor-led training (ILT), instructor guides are the collective, step-by-step "lesson plans" that an instructor uses to organize and run a training course. ■ An IG generally contains a prep-to-teach component, a course agenda, the core content, directions for facilitating learning activities, and copies of visuals and handouts. ■ An IG includes more content and more precise directions than an instructor notes.
☐	Job Aids	■ Job aids are often given as "take-aways" to help participants continue to use and develop new skills when they return to the workplace. ■ They are short, simple, directive but user-friendly tools usually presented as a simple one-page handout, a laminated "Quick Reference," or even a small reminder card (that can be posted in a participant's work area).
☐	Journals	■ Notebooks may be given to participants for journaling, an instructional method whereby participants reflect on some topic, question, or events and record their reflections in writing. ■ Time should be built into the agenda for participants to make entries into their journals.
☐	Media Files	■ Instructors and/or participants may use audio, video, or data files.
☐	Observation Checklist	■ If a learning program focuses on learning a process or procedure, it is helpful to create an observation checklist that specifies behaviors that make up that process or procedure (in the correct sequence, if applicable). ■ Observation checklists provide an objective standard by which feedback can be given on a participant's performance. ■ Instructors or participants can fill out observation checklists – for example, participants can work in groups of three with two participants practicing the skill and a third acting as observer and completing the checklist.
☐	Participant Guide (PG)	■ A participant guide (PG) is a collection of materials used by participants during a training course or after a course for reference (in the latter case, the term reference guide – RG – is often used). ■ Participant guides contain an agenda or course map, the core content (perhaps as copies of presentation slides), copies of pertinent articles (copyright permission must be secured), and suggestions for further study. ■ Some participant guides are developed as workbooks, with areas for participants to write down their thoughts or to complete activities. ■ PGs are often paper-based, but they can be electronic documents or even a course database.

Materials	Notes
☐ Posters	• Posters can be created to capture or illustrate key information, models, and processes. • If special printers are available (in-house or through a copy or office services store), posters can be made from PowerPoint slides.
☐ Post-test	• A post-test is an assessment instrument that measures how well participants achieved the learning objectives of a learning program. • Post-tests should focus on measuring the achievement of learning objectives. Each objective should have a range of associated questions. • NASBA Standards require a posttest score of 70% or better to award CPE credit for self-study programs. • A post-assessment does not have to be a traditional test, it can be an observation of performance or some other means that verifies achievement of learning objectives.
☐ Presentation Slides	• PowerPoint slides are common in instructor-led learning programs, whether traditional or virtual classroom based. • The quickest way to create participant materials to accompany a lecture/presentation is to print handouts directly from PowerPoint. • Overhead transparencies are rarely used instead of presentation slides. Transparencies can be made from PowerPoint files.
☐ Pre-test	• A pre-test is a diagnostic assessment given to participants either before or at the start of training to gauge their relevant prior knowledge or skills. • Pre-tests are used with post-tests to help measure learning gain.
☐ Pre-work (pre-read)	• Pre-work is the commonly used term for a preparatory assignment sent to participants prior to the conduct of a learning program. • Pre-work often contains information that participants should read before coming to training (pre-work consisting entirely of reading material is often called a "pre-read"). • One common use of pre-work is to give participants the fundamental facts and concepts that they will apply during the learning event. Another use is to give some form of self-assessment to help participants identify relevant learning needs.
☐ Reference (or Resource) Guide	• A reference guide (RG) is a collection of core content and suggestions for further study. • A reference guide is a form of participant guide that is intended to be a repository of course content that participants can consult as needed after a training course.

CONTINUED ——————— **Develop T-02**

St. Charles
Consulting Group
© 2010

Materials	Notes
☐ **Research Tools (databases, intranet, Internet)**	▪ Learning program content (primary and supplemental content) can be stored in repositories. This relies on participants having computers and network access in the classroom. ▪ Technical support must be available in case of connection problems, etc. ▪ These tools are useful in learning programs that focus on research and data gathering as a precursor to problem solving.
☐ **Self-assessment**	▪ A self-assessment is a formal or informal instrument or activity that a participant uses individually to gauge his or her own knowledge or skill level. Self-assessments are also often used to help individuals learn about their own preferences or tendencies. The Myers-Briggs Type Indicator (MBTI) is an example of this sort of self-assessment instrument. It has become a somewhat common design practice to have some sort of self-assessment either as pre-work to a learning program or as an early activity within the learning program itself.
☐ **Timers**	▪ One of the biggest challenges in delivering learning programs is managing time. Timers help instructors and participants stay on the agenda. ▪ Timers are very useful during activities, particularly ones that involve discussion. ▪ Participants will tolerate straying from the agenda in a training event, as long as it does not push back the stop time at the end of the day.
☐ **Video**	▪ Video can be presented, usually from a DVD or a digital file. ▪ Video is useful for observing processes and procedures because instructors can pause and rewind as needed. ▪ Queue videos up to the proper starting point before a session begins and test visual quality and volume. ▪ Video cameras can be used to record participant performance and used during one-on-one feedback sessions.

Develop T-02

Directions: Authentic practice is a key ingredient to adult learning, and what makes learning authentic is the context – the situation in which the activity adopts. Program developers often create scenarios to use in role plays and simulations. Below are some simple guidelines to help you in this task.

General Guidelines for Creating Scenarios

1. **Focus on a problem or dilemma.** When writing a scenario, start with a problem or a dilemma that requires a decision. Then add only those characters and situational details needed to create a scene participants can visualize.

2. **Keep it short and simple.** Although a scenario presents a dramatic situation, use a straightforward presentation style. If you are presenting your scenario in writing, be simple and clear. Keep sentences short, with subjects and verbs close together, and use simple present tense to describe actions.

3. **Make it real.** Keeping it simple does not mean leaving out specifics. You need to paint a picture in the participant's mind: to do so, you need some tangible details.

4. **Keep it open-ended.** There should technically be no correct answer, although one option may be more appropriate than others. (Why this option is more appropriate should be explained in the feedback.) The learning comes from the individual weighing and evaluating the information given, making a decision, and experiencing the consequences of that decision.

General Guidelines for Creating Role-Plays

1. **Use generic names and situations.** Use names like Lee, Terry, Kelly that are not gender specific. Do not make the character sketches too complex. Participants are not professional actors.

2. **Define the role's motivation.** Define the role's motivation in terms of the central problem or dilemma (see above). How does this person feel about the problem? What does he or she think the cause or likely solution might be?

3. **Provide talking points not scripts.** Do not script out a role. Provide some talking points, some general parameters to make the conversation real, and let the role-player use language and add details appropriate to the situation.

4. **Describe the situation clearly and concisely.** Write a one-paragraph (two at most) description of the situation in which role-players find themselves (follow the guidelines above for writing the scenario). Put this description on a handout or a presentation slide and give participants sufficient time to read and study it before the role-play begins.

5. **Include quality control.** The success of a role-play often depends on participants' commitment to making it worthwhile. For difficult, content-heavy roles, instructors or facilitators could play the part. For small-group role-playing, where participants are in pairs or trios, make sure instructors move about the room and monitor the activity so that participants maintain focus.

Develop T-03

Directions: Job aids are designed to help people perform a procedure correctly and more quickly. They are short, succinct, and action-oriented. If you are creating job aids, follow these guidelines.

1. **Use a template.**
   - If you are going to create more than one job aid – and it is very likely you will – you need a **template**. If job aids are designed to help people "in the act," then they should not require the user to understand a new look and feel for each job aid.
   - Imagine the "in the act" effectiveness of a stop sign if each stop sign on each road were a different color and had a different shape!

2. **Focus on <u>do</u>.**
   - Job aids must explicitly and clearly answer the question: **"What do I do?"**
   - Make the title of your job aid an explicit statement of what the person uses the job aid to do.

3. **Keep it short, simple, and concrete.**
   - More than any other communication or learning vehicle, a job aid needs to follow a **clear concise approach**.
   - Limit the amount of information and use straightforward – but grammatically correct – language. Avoid overly conceptual language or ambiguous terms, and do not use colloquialisms or contractions.
   - Your job aid should sound like one of two things: 1) step-by-step instructions from an expert practitioner, or 2) sensible advice from a business mentor.

4. **Use bullets or numbers for a reason.**
   - If you are listing items that are of relatively equal importance and have no set order, **use bullets**. If you are listing procedural steps that do have a set sequence, use numbers.

5. **Put catchwords in bold.**
   - Put important words in **boldface**, followed by an explanation as appropriate.

6. **Organize graphically.**
   - Organize your job aid so that people can take it in **at a glance**. Ideally, readers should be able to retain a mental representation of the information on your job aid. Use clear, meaningful labels.

7. **Provide an example or model.**
   - In most cases job aids should be designed for self-study – individuals working alone to accomplish a task.
   - Self-study thrives on **good examples** and **clear models** to follow. Explanation of concepts is not enough.

8. **Remove any dependencies on or references to other materials.**
   - As stand-alone pieces, job aids should not contain any references to other materials or job aids. All content should be **self-explanatory** – there are no prerequisites for a job aid! If you are creating a job aid from existing course content, make sure you remove references and change wording to make sure your job aid really stands on its own.

Develop T-04

Directions: Self-studies require a final examination or posttest. If you are developing simple test items (multiple choice and true/false), consult these guidelines.

General Guidelines for Developing Simple Test Items

1. Take time to plan. Before you start writing test items, determine first the key content you want to address and then the number, type, range, and "thinking level" of test items needed to enable the desired learning.
2. Consider how long it should take a learner to complete all the objective test items in this module. A basic rule is to allow 30-45 seconds for each test item.
3. Try to address a range of "thinking levels" in your items – simple recall of facts; comprehension of concepts; recognition of cause and effect; ability to compare and contrast; application of principles to a new situation.
4. Make sure the item focuses on "need to know" information. Give each item the "So what?" test by asking yourself whether knowing or not knowing the answer would make a significant difference in the person's competence in the area being tested.
5. Provide a range of questions for each learning objective or key content point that you are testing.
6. Put general directions at the beginning and put section-specific directions with those sections.
7. Keep items of the same type (multiple choice, true/false) together and provide directions before each section – each grouping of types.
8. Group questions together based on topic or learning objective.
9. In general, move from less challenging to more challenging items.
10. Keep all parts of the item – directions, question, response options – in one view or page. For each item, make sure learners see everything they need in one view – no scrolling and no page turning.
11. Questions that include a figure, graph, picture, or some other stimulus should follow a standard format – for example, picture to the right of the question. Make sure the directions, question, picture, and response options fit in one view or on one page.
12. Do not create items by taking language verbatim from the instructional materials. Rephrase the content as needed.
13. Do not make answering one item correctly a prerequisite for answering the next (or a later) item.
14. Check and double-check your questions for any ambiguity or hint of ambiguity.
15. Make sure the correct answers in the multiple-choice options are distributed equally and occur in a random pattern.
16. Make sure there are about the same number of true and false statements – in fact, since people tend to select "true" more often, consider having slightly more "false" statements.
17. Give all necessary information in the question or statement.
18. Use full sentences – complete questions for multiple-choice items and complete statements for true/false items.
19. Avoid items based on opinions. If an item is based on opinion or authority, indicate in the question or statement whose statement or what authority is to be used to answer the question.
20. Do not ask trick questions.
21. Avoid "all," "always," "never," "usually," and similar words.

——————— CONTINUED ——————— **Develop T-05**

22. Avoid negative words like "not," "except," or "incorrect" in the introductory question or statement. People look at questions, they do not read them: Make your test items a valid assessment of people's knowledge, not their ability to read carefully.
    − If you must use a negative word like *not*, emphasize the word by putting it in italics or all caps.
23. Ask one question at a time. Do not use compound questions in your items.
24. Write your test item in the most direct and simplest form feasible.
    − Use simple, direct language.
    − Keep verb forms simple.
    − Keep subjects and verbs close together.
    − Avoid long introductory phrases – get to your subject and verb quickly.
    − Include only enough information to enable the learner to formulate an answer.
25. Avoid humor – in fact, avoid anything that may distract, frustrate, or annoy anyone in your target audience.
26. Most important, let someone else review the test items before distributing them to your audience. This reviewer should be knowledgeable in the subject matter covered by the test items but not involved in writing the test items.

Multiple-choice Items
▪ Multiple-choice questions have a question and typically three to four response options. Of these response options, one is the correct answer and the other incorrect answers are often called "distracters."

Creating the Question
1. Pose multiple-choice questions as complete questions rather than sentence-completion types.
    CORRECT: "Which of the following is the first step in the xyz process?"
    INCORRECT: "The first step in the xyz process is …?"
2. In multiple-choice questions, start with the question word – Which, Who, What, When, Where, How, Why.
    CORRECT: "Which of the following is the first step in the xyz process"?
    INCORRECT: "In the xyz process which of the following is the first step?"
3. When testing knowledge of definitions, put the word to be defined in the question and alternative definitions in the options.
    CORRECT: Which of these is the correct definition of *target audience*?
    ❑ Those who have expertise in the subject matter
    ❑ Those who design the program of learning
    ❑ Those who provide funding for the program of learning
    ❑ Those who participate in the program of learning
    INCORRECT: Which of the following terms describes "those who participate in the program of learning"?
    ❑ Content experts
    ❑ Instructional designers
    ❑ Sponsors
    ❑ Target audience

——————— CONTINUED ——————— **Develop T-05**

Creating Response Options

1. Make sure only one correct option exists.

2. Make all response options approximately the same length.

3. Make all response options the same grammatical form – for example, all nouns phrases or all complete sentences.

4. Avoid "all of the above" and "none of the above" response options.

5. Word response options in the positive, not the negative.

> **CORRECT:** Which of these is an appropriate guideline for creating a true/false question?
> - ❑ Test just one concept
> - ❑ …
> - ❑ …
>
> **INCORRECT:** Which of these is an appropriate guideline for creating a true/false question?
> - ❑ Do not test more than one concept
> - ❑ …
> - ❑ …

6. Arrange response options in a logical order if one exists – for example, if options are numbers, present in ascending or descending order; if options are dates, present in chronological order.

7. Make sure response options do not overlap.

> **CORRECT:** At what age level does schizophrenia appear most frequently?
> - ❑ Under age 15
> - ❑ Between ages 15 and 35
> - ❑ Between ages 36 and 45
> - ❑ Over age 65
>
> **INCORRECT:** At what age level does schizophrenia appear most frequently?
> - ❑ In persons younger than 15
> - ❑ In persons younger than 35
> - ❑ In persons over 40
> - ❑ In persons over 65

Guidelines for Creating Distractors

1. Distractors must be incorrect, but they must be plausible. If you cannot come up with three plausible distractors, use two.

2. Use anticipated errors – common misconceptions people have about the topic – as distractors. Addressing common misconceptions is an effective instructional strategy.

3. Use statements that are true in and of themselves but are not the correct answer for <u>this</u> question. In other words, do not use "made up" information in a distractor.

———————————— CONTINUED ———————————— **Develop T-05**

St. Charles
© 2010   Consulting Group

Common Mistakes

The following are some very common mistakes test item developers make:

- Response options are antonyms or opposites of each other. This can either eliminate the other two response options or unfairly distract the person from the correct answer.
- Distractors are so implausible that they are obviously not correct.
- The correct answer is the longest response option in a multiple-choice question.
- A common "give away" in true/false questions is that true statements tend to be longer than false ones.
- The correct answer to this question was revealed in a previous question.
- Identical or very similar words or phrases appear in both the question and the correct response.
- The developer unwittingly provides grammatical clues between the introductory question and the correct answer.

True/False Items

1. True/false questions have a statement and two response options labeled simply "True" and "False" (always in that order) – for example:

    The purpose of a needs assessment is to produce learning objectives.

    ❑ True
    ❑ False

2. True/false statements must be unequivocally true or false.

3. Test only one concept. Avoid the use of two concepts when one is true and the other is false.

4. Do not make a true statement false simply by inserting "not" or some other negative word or phrase.

Directions: Whether your delivery strategy is Internet-based self-study or classroom-based group study, odds are that you will be communicating content to instructors and participants in written words. Clear, concise, sensible writing is an often-overlooked but critical skill for program developers. This guide covers general standards of style for paper-based and electronic documents. Whether you use this particular guide or another is not so important. What is important is having a guide, particularly when there are multiple writers of content. Getting your team to follow a consistent style results in less re-work.

Grammar and Punctuation Guidelines

- Body text should be flush left, ragged right. Do not indent paragraphs.
- Separate paragraphs by one row or space.
- Use <u>one</u> space after a period or colon.
- To avoid "dating" your materials, state dates in absolute terms – for example, "the events of the spring of 2002," not "the events or last spring" or "recent events such as ..."
- In body text, the numbers one through ten are spelled out in full; thereafter use numerals.

Guidelines for Bulleted Text

- Capitalize the first word in a bulleted list.
- Do not use a period at the end of a bulleted item unless that item is a complete sentence.
- Do not use numbers or letters in place of bullets unless a definite sequence is required.
- Use the same part of speech or syntax (nouns, phrases, sentences) for each bulleted item – for example, do not mix complete and incomplete sentences.

    Incorrect

    In performing this task, you have three goals:
    - *Verify that the start button is depressed.*
    - *Keep the power usage within acceptable limits.*
    - *Accurate error detection.*

    Correct

    In performing this task, you have three goals:
    - *Verify that the start button is depressed.*
    - *Keep the power usage within acceptable limits.*
    - *Detect errors accurately.*

Making Points Clearly, Concisely, and Forcibly

- Within each paragraph, state your main point in the <u>first</u> sentence and use the following sentences for explanation, examples, evidence, and elaboration.
    - Basically, construct your document so that a reader can read only the first sentence of each paragraph and still gain a firm understanding of the key points. Proofread your document by reading just the first sentence of each paragraph to see if you have achieved this goal.

—————————— CONTINUED —————————— **Develop T-06**

St. Charles
Consulting Group

© 2010

Making Points Clearly, Concisely, and Forcibly (continued)

- Keep paragraphs to no more than a few brief sentences.
- Use present tense – for example, "This lesson presents …" not "This lesson will present …"
- Use active voice – for example, "The team leader <u>completes</u> these steps …" not "These steps <u>are completed</u> by the team leader …"
- Omit punctuation for abbreviations and acronyms, and do not use contractions.
- Keep your writing simple and strong.
  - Delete pretentious words and substitute simpler ones – for example, do not <u>initiate</u> things, <u>start</u> them; do not <u>terminate</u> things, <u>end</u> them. Avoid legalistic expressions and jargon as well.
  - Check for and eliminate redundancy, which often appears in doubling expressions such as "importance and significance," or "functions and roles."
  - Avoid wordy expressions – for example, change "make a choice" to "choose"; change "provide a reference to" to "refer to."
  - Avoid the unnecessary use of "-ion" nouns in phrases – for example, change "We want the participation of all members" to "We want all members to participate." In general, do not turn verbs into nouns in an effort to sound more "business-like."

Final Reminders

- Use Print Preview to check how your document looks – especially how content breaks across pages. Do this before printing out large documents and before sending electronic documents to reviewers, etc.
- Run spell-checker on your documents – draft or final – before sending them to anyone.

CPE FIELD GUIDE —— Brand, Copyright & Trademark Guidelines

Directions: Use this checklist as you review training materials for brand, copyright, and trademark compliance. Each item on this list **must have a check** next to it in order for the training to be considered in compliance.

Branding (font, formatting, graphics, icons, color palette, CPA firm logo) & Copyright

☐ The correct logo is prominently displayed on the front cover of training guides, slides, binders, and folders.

☐ If the training is for internal purposes, the training materials use the CPA firm color palette, graphics, and iconography according to brand standards.

☐ The training materials use approved templates (for slides or training guides), fonts, and formatting.

☐ Proper CPA firm terminology is used when referring to service offerings, products, classifications, offices, initiatives, and so forth,

☐ The training adheres to the CPA firm style guide and the Associated Press Style Guide for spelling, grammar, and punctuation.

☐ An abbreviated CPA firm copyright statement is displayed on the footer of every training item (handouts, training guides, slides, evaluation forms, etc.)

☐ The training materials have been checked for any graphics, icons, pictures, diagrams, images, flowcharts, artwork, comic strips, quotations, passages, articles, book excerpts, citations, or media clips (such as audio, video, or multimedia). Every item not from an internal or open source (such as websites that do not limit how others use their content or images) has the following:

- A signed, up-to-date copyright agreement between the CPA firm and the owner of the content stating that it is OK for the company to use the item in the training materials.
- A copyright statement, as specified in the agreement.

There is a signed, current copyright agreement on file for each instance of externally created material that is used in the training.

☐ A special copyright statement is displayed along with the externally created material, as specified in the copyright agreement.

Trademark (companies and their product names and services)

☐ References to proprietary product names or services also include the company name and the registered trademark symbol. Check the references to make sure they are spelled, spaced, and punctuated exactly like that company's own references to its products or services (for example, "Hewlett Packard LaserJet 5®" -- not "HP Laserjet 5"). **Note:** Not every reference requires the registered trademark symbol. As a rule of thumb, using the trademark symbol the first time you refer to a company's product or service and then periodically thereafter (first instance on a page, whenever it is used in a title or section heading, and so forth) is sufficient.

Develop T-07

Directions: Use this guide to help you evaluate a program that has been developed. The first section addresses CPE requirements, the second instructional quality, and the third the appropriateness to your audience and environment. Questions answered "no" should suggest revisions that need to be made.

Part A: Does this program meet minimum CPE requirements?

(Note: For the program to meet CPE standards, you must be able to answer yes to every question below.)

A1.	Does this program of learning clearly state learning objectives – the level of knowledge or skill that participants are expected to achieve upon completion?	☐ Yes ☐ No
A2.	Does this program of learning specify a program level: basic, intermediate, advanced, update, or overview?	☐ Yes ☐ No
A3.	Is the recommended amount of CPE credit for this program of learning clearly stated?	☐ Yes ☐ No
A4.	Does the program identify the prerequisite knowledge, education, or experience that participants must have or do before beginning this learning program to achieve the desired outcomes?	☐ Yes ☐ No
A5.	Does the program identify any advanced preparation – pre-work, pre-readings, and so forth – that participants must complete beforehand?	☐ Yes ☐ No
A6.	Are instructional methods – how the course is delivered – appropriate to the stated learning objectives?	☐ Yes ☐ No
A7.	Were individuals with content expertise and knowledge of instructional design involved in the development of the course?	☐ Yes ☐ No
A8.	Were the program materials reviewed by qualified persons other than the persons who developed them for: 1) technical accuracy, 2) currency, and 3) appropriate design to meet learning objectives?	☐ Yes ☐ No
A9.	Are the instructors qualified in terms of program content and instructional methods?	☐ Yes ☐ No
A10.	Does the learning program include an "effective means of evaluating the learning activity with respect to content and presentation, as well a mechanism for participants to assess whether learning objectives were met"?	☐ Yes ☐ No

Comments:

Part B: Is the learning program instructionally sound?

B1.	Do learning objectives clearly state what participants will learn or do as a result of this learning program?	☐ Yes ☐ No
B2.	Is each learning activity clearly tied to specific learning objective?	☐ Yes ☐ No
B3.	Does each learning activity address relevant, realistic situations and include: 1) reference to workplace responsibilities or 2) how the new knowledge and skill will be applied to the work??	☐ Yes ☐ No
B4.	Do the first and last activities make a powerful first impression and a meaningful last impression?	☐ Yes ☐ No
B5.	Is the content technically accurate and up to date?	☐ Yes ☐ No
B6.	Is there a content outline – course agenda, course map – that clearly conveys to participants how the learning program is organized and how modules or topics relate to each other?	☐ Yes ☐ No
B7.	Is the program well organized – that is, it follows a sequence and has a distribution of emphasis that makes sense given the subject matter?	☐ Yes ☐ No
B8.	Is the program "chunked" appropriately – that is, broken up into easily "digestible" or "learnable" pieces?	☐ Yes ☐ No
B9.	Is the program organized so that successive topics vary in delivery approach – for example, do lectures or reading passages alternate with hands-on activities?	☐ Yes ☐ No
B10.	Are transitions used effectively to help participants move from one topic to the next, seeing the connection between the two?	☐ Yes ☐ No
B11.	Are there periodic summaries to help participants consolidate what they have just learned before moving on to new topics?	☐ Yes ☐ No
B12.	Are instructional materials – documents, visual aids – neat, clean, well written, and visually appealing?	☐ Yes ☐ No
B13.	Does the learning program employ instructional methods that spark and maintain participant interest?	☐ Yes ☐ No
B14.	Is content presented in multiple ways – for example, text, graphics, sound – to suit different learning styles?	☐ Yes ☐ No
B15.	Are there sufficient opportunities for participants to practice what is being learned? And does each participant have the opportunity to practice each skill?	☐ Yes ☐ No
B16.	Are opportunities for immediate feedback – instructor/expert and peer feedback – paired with practice opportunities?	☐ Yes ☐ No

B17.	Are group interactions or activities well designed – that is, do they provide for adequate set-up and debrief?	☐ Yes ☐ No
B18.	Are suggestions provided for further study?	☐ Yes ☐ No

Comments:

Part C: Is the learning program appropriate to your audience and environment?

C1.	Are objectives appropriate to the intended audience – for example, are they at the right level, and are they attainable in the time period allotted?	☐ Yes ☐ No
C2.	Is the content – text, graphics, audio/visual materials, and so forth – inclusive in terms of gender, culture, and other participant characteristics?	☐ Yes ☐ No
C3.	Are there enough relevant examples to help participants understand how to apply what they learned to their own jobs and how it will benefit them?	☐ Yes ☐ No
C4.	Do summaries not only review what has been covered but also emphasize how the newly learned content can be applied to the participants' own situation?	☐ Yes ☐ No
C5.	Is the material presented at the right level for the participants?	☐ Yes ☐ No
C6.	Is there a clear indication of how the program content directly relates to the needs (the jobs) of the participants?	☐ Yes ☐ No
C7.	Do the program materials employ delivery approaches that suit the facilities and resources in your learning environment?	☐ Yes ☐ No
C8.	Does the learning program employ delivery approaches that match the participants' work situation – for example, if participants work in a team-based environment does the program employ collaborative, team-based learning activities?	☐ Yes ☐ No
C9.	Are there sufficient opportunities for participants to present and share their own knowledge of the topic in interaction with others?	☐ Yes ☐ No

Comments:

Develop T-08

CPE FIELD GUIDE ———————— Developer Review Form

Directions: The lead developer should use this form to confirm that design & development of the program was done in conformance with all CPE standards.*

Program Name: _____   **Date(s):** _____

I, the lead developer, confirm that the following standards were met in developing this program:

☐ **Learning objectives** were determined to maintain or enhance the professional competency of CPAs. They focus on the participant, and they clearly articulate the specific knowledge, skills, and abilities that will be achieved as a direct result of the program..

☐ **Learning objectives** accurately represent the program and match the program content. There is little to no content in the program material that is not covered by the learning objectives.

☐ The appropriate **program level** (overview, basic, intermediate, advanced, update) has been assigned, and it matches the program content.

☐ The **prerequisites** in education, experience, and/or advance preparation of participants are clearly stated, and the program is consistent with the requirements.

☐ The **program** is consistent with educational methodologies and instructional methods suitable for the method of delivery (group live, group internet-based, self-study).

☐ The **program** and all of the supporting materials are current, technically accurate, and effectively designed.

☐ The **program** was developed by one or more individuals qualified in the subject matter and familiar with principles of instructional design.

☐ The program was **reviewed** for currency, accuracy, and sufficiency by an individual qualified in the subject matter.

☐ Anyone in a **reviewer** role was not involved in authoring any of the program content.

☐ **CPE credits** were calculated correctly (based on a 50-minute contact hour, rounded down to the nearest one-half credit (after the first full credit).

☐ **CPE credits** were assigned to the appropriate field(s) of study.

Printed Name: _____

Signature: _____

Date: _____

* If the CPE program is in the self-study format, there are a number of additional CPE standards that apply. These self-study requirements are <u>not</u> included in the **CPE Field Guide**.

Develop T-09

CPE FIELD GUIDE ———————— Technical Review Form

Directions: The independent technical reviewer should use this form to confirm that design & development of the program was done in conformance with all CPE standards.

Program Name: _____   **Date(s):** _____

I, the technical reviewer, confirm the following:

☐ I am knowledgeable of this program's subject matter.

☐ I was not involved in authoring any of the program content.

☐ I reviewed the program for currency, accuracy, and sufficiency, and this review took place before release of the program (either the first time or on significant revision).

☐ In my opinion, the program content is current, technically accurate, and it addresses the stated learning objectives.

Printed Name: _____

Signature: _____

Date: _____

Develop T-10

Directions: Use this observation checklist to guide your evaluation of a pilot test of a developed learning program before it is delivered or rolled out to the target audience.

Preliminary Qualification

1.	**Brand and copyright compliance**. Learning materials comply with brand, copyright, and trademark requirements.	☐ Yes ☐ No
2.	**Technical accuracy and timeliness**. Learning materials are technically accurate and up to date.	☐ Yes ☐ No

Qualitative Observations

3.	**Appearance**. Learning materials look neat and clean when printed out and photocopied, and they are free from spelling and grammatical errors.	☐ Weak ☐ OK ☐ Strong
4.	**Quantity**. The right amount of content is presented given the allotted training time.	☐ Weak ☐ OK ☐ Strong
5.	**Level**. The content is at the right level for participants given their background and experience. (It does not oversimplify or talk over their heads.)	☐ Weak ☐ OK ☐ Strong
6.	**Purpose**. Participants get a clear picture of their goals – what to expect from this learning program and what this learning program expects of them.	☐ Weak ☐ OK ☐ Strong
7.	**Module organization**. The organization makes sense for this topic – modules are clearly organized around learning goals or key steps in the overall process.	☐ Weak ☐ OK ☐ Strong
8.	**Sequence**. The content is presented in a sequence that is logical, practical, appealing, and helps participants build skills.	☐ Weak ☐ OK ☐ Strong
9.	**Emphasis**. It is clear that content presented is essential to the job and any supplemental content is clearly marked as "nice to know."	☐ Weak ☐ OK ☐ Strong
10.	**Relevance**. It is clear how the content, activities, and examples relate to the target audience's job role & responsibilities.	☐ Weak ☐ OK ☐ Strong
11.	**Challenge**. Participants find content and activities meaningful, engaging, and appropriately challenging.	☐ Weak ☐ OK ☐ Strong
12.	**Variety**. The learning program provides enough variety in instructional methods to maintain participant interest.	☐ Weak ☐ OK ☐ Strong
13.	**Practice**. There is enough time set aside for practice so participants can measure their progress.	☐ Weak ☐ OK ☐ Strong

——————— CONTINUED ——————— **Develop T-11**

Qualitative Observations (continued)

14. **Feedback**. Practice opportunities are paired with feedback so participants hear, see, and recognize what they do well and what they need to improve.	☐ Weak ☐ OK ☐ Strong
15. **Activity design**. Learning activities make sense given the learning objective for each activity and the delivery environment resources.	☐ Weak ☐ OK ☐ Strong
16. **Environment**. The learning environment – classroom or work area in which training takes place – is physically and psychologically conducive to learning.	☐ Weak ☐ OK ☐ Strong
17. **Transitions and debriefs**. Transitions and debriefs help participants check their progress, link new to prior learning, and see how components fit together.	☐ Weak ☐ OK ☐ Strong
18. **Timing**. The learning program is the right length, and activities stay on schedule without feeling rushed.	☐ Weak ☐ OK ☐ Strong

Comments:

Develop T-11

Directions: Use this form to calculate the amount of CPE credits to be granted by field of study.

Course Name: _____ **Date(s):** _____

Program Modules	Field(s) of Study Code	Minutes of Instruction					
Total Minutes							
CPE Credits (divide by 50, round down to nearest half-hour*)							

Number of credits eligible for:							
	Ethics						
	Employee Benefits						
	Fraud						
	SEC						
	Yellow Book (A&A)						
	Yellow Book (Government)						

* - most jurisdictions allow half credits after the
first full credit has been earned in a given learning activity.

Page: _____

Develop T-12

© 2010

St. Charles
Consulting Group

Directions: The following are the 23 fields of study (FOS) recognized in the NASBA CPE Standards. All learning content must be assigned to one or more FOS in order to quality for CPE credit.

No.	Field of Study	Description
1.	Accounting	Accounting research; financial statements & reports; measurement, recognition & presentation of specific financial statement items; SEC practice; accounting services for small business; accounting – general; forensic accounting.
2.	Accounting (Governmental)	Governmental accounting and reporting; government accounting and reporting – specialized; forensic accounting.
3.	Auditing	Auditing research; auditing and electronic data processing (EDP); substantive audit procedures; independent auditors' reports; study and evaluation of internal control; auditing – general; forensic auditing.
4.	Auditing (Governmental)	Government auditing – general and specialized; forensic auditing.
5.	Administrative Practice	Management advisory services (MAS) practice skills; MAS engagement management; planning & control systems: human resources development & organizational; personal financial planning.
6.	Social Environment of Business	Planning & control systems: manufacturing marketing, research & development, finance, management information systems; other management advisory services.
7.	Regulatory Ethics	The necessary ethical background knowledge required to adhere to rules and regulations of state licensing bodies, other governmental entities, membership associations, and other professional organizations or bodies.
8.	Business Law	Subjects related to the legal system with special emphasis upon its relationship to business and the practice of accounting
9.	Business Management & Organization	Subjects related to the management of an organization, including information systems, organizational structures, planning & administrative practices.
10.	Finance	Subjects related to specific financial management of an organization including budgeting & asset management, buying and selling businesses, contracting goods & services ,and foreign operations.
11.	Management Advisory Services	Subjects related to key processes, achieving efficiencies, improving cash flow, and maintaining profitability
12.	Marketing	Subjects related to the examination of market analysis methods & their use to develop an organization's product/service mix and the integration of the communication, distribution, and pricing strategies to achieve goals.
13.	Behavior Ethics	Subjects related to general professional ethics programs including, but not limited to ethics & professional conduct, ethical practice in business, personal ethics, ethical decision-making, corporate ethics.
14.	Communications	Subjects related to communication including but not limited to interview techniques, business writing, business presentations, group dynamics, public relations, group process management, counseling.
15.	Personal Development	Subjects related to the general development of personal skills including but not limited to principle-centered leadership, career planning, time management.
16.	Personnel / HR	Subjects related to how organizations attract, motivate, develop, and retain employees; the functional areas of human resource management; integration of HR functions into human resource management system(s).
17.	Computer Science	Subjects related to networking, computer hardware, system software, application software – such as web browsers, word processing, spreadsheets, database management systems, presentation software.
18.	Economics	Studies related to the principles of pricing, stabilization, supply and demand, employment theory, fiscal policy banking systems, monetary policy, economic growth, and fundamentals of the international economy
19.	Mathematics	Subjects related to the fundamental concepts of mathematical problem-solving including, but not limited to algebra, geometry, calculus.
20.	Production	Subjects related to production management including production scheduling, inventory control, standards for pay and production, and quality control.
21.	Specialized Knowledge & Applications	Subjects related to a specialized skill set and/or specialized industries (such as not-for-profit organizations, health care, oil & gas).
22.	Statistics	Subjects related to multivariate probability distributions, estimation of parameters, hypothesis testing, linear models, analysis of variance, analysis of enumerative data, and nonparametric statistics.
23.	Taxes	Subjects related to tax compliance (tax return preparation & review and IRS examinations, ruling requests & protests) and tax planning (applying tax rules to prospective transactions & understanding the tax implications of unusual or complex transactions).

Develop T-13

Deliver

*It usually takes me more than three weeks
to prepare a good impromptu speech.*

— Mark Twain *(Author and Humorist)*

Directions: Use this form to document the members of the program's instructor team and their specific qualifications as: current in the subject matter, proficient in the use of appropriate instructional methods, and skilled in communicating effectively and providing an environment conducive to learning.

LEAD INSTRUCTOR(S)				
Name	**Program Responsibilities**	**Qualifications**	**CPA?**	
			Y	N
			Y	N
			Y	N
			Y	N
OTHER INSTRUCTOR(S)				
Name(s)	**Program Responsibilities**	**Qualifications**	**CPA?**	
			Y	N
			Y	N
			Y	N
			Y	N
			Y	N
			Y	N
			Y	N
			Y	N
			Y	N
			Y	N

Deliver T-01

Directions: Share these guidelines with your classroom instructors so that they can more effectively prepare to teach classroom-based learning programs.

Preparing Before Class

1. **Understand the course design, goals, and objectives.** Understanding these will help you determine the right pace and emphasis.

2. **Review all instructor materials.** A high-level review of all the instructor materials helps you understand the flow of the course and how your assigned content fits in.

3. **Focus on your assigned material.** As you read your assigned content determine the top three to five "need to know" points.

4. **Talk to your co-instructors.** Work with your co-instructors to determine teaching assignments and how you will interact in the classroom. Planning ahead of time will make the material appear seamless and will help you avoid contradicting your co-instructors.

5. **Create supporting media.** Create your supporting media – flipcharts, presentation slides, handouts – ahead of time so you can focus on your teaching.

6. **Make the material your own.** Personalize the material based on your experience. Put it in your own words; add your own examples, experiences, and analogies.

7. **Make your own outline or notes.** Use an outline or make comments in the instructor guide to include your examples, analogies, timing, discussion or debriefing questions, and any special material needs.

8. **Understand the equipment.** Make sure you learn ahead of time how to use the equipment and whom to contact if there are problems.

Presenting Content

1. **Mix it up. Use a variety of media and methods.** Use flipcharts, whiteboards, even participants – alter the view periodically so that participants are not always looking at presentation slides.

2. **Give participants a reason to listen.** Make your instruction participant-centered not content-centered. The question to answer is, "Am I making it meaningful for this audience?" not "Am I covering the subject matter?"

3. **Highlight the agenda.** Use a posted agenda as a road map to: 1) summarize the current topic in terms of the overall course goals, and 2) make transitions between topics.

4. **Make the connections.** For every content topic or activity covered, summarize the key points and state how that topic or activity relates to: 1) what they have learned, 2) what they will learn, and 3) what they do on the job.

──────── CONTINUED ──────── **Deliver T-02**

Presenting Content (continued)

5. **Share stories and experiences.** Participants appreciate your expertise and enjoy hearing these stories. They learn a lot from both successes and failures. Remember to ask participants to share their own stories and lessons learned.

6. **Repeat and restate key points.** The most effective way to teach knowledge-based information (names, labels, facts) is by repetition and restatement. Simple repetition is also an effective attention-gainer.

7. **Look for ways to make it more interactive.** As you prepare ask yourself, "Do the participants already know or have experience with this content?" If the answer is yes, think of ways to make it more interactive through discussions or activities.

Facilitating Discussions

1. **Prepare for your discussions.** Determine what questions you will ask and any follow-up questions or examples you can use to guide participants. Think of questions that allow them to learn from each other.

2. **Ask good questions.** Use open-ended, thought-provoking questions to encourage participants to offer their own insights and become more engaged in the material. Ask one question at a time and give participants time to hear the question and formulate a response.

3. **Do not show the slide, reveal it!** Instead of showing a slide and walking through the contents, pique participant curiosity by stating something like this: "The next slide lists the top three most common errors new consultants make during the client interview. Can anyone make an informed guess about what they are?" Slides often provide the "correct" answers to many discussion questions. Only show that slide after you have given participants a chance to answer. If all the points came out in the discussion, you do not need to show the slide at all.

4. **Call on groups.** If you ask an open-ended question and receive no response, call on groups. For example, say, "Let's hear from the back of the room," or "Let's hear from someone at this table." By doing so you encourage participants to respond without singling out individuals.

5. **Make sure everyone can hear.** Ask participants to repeat their question or comment, or restate the question yourself as an introduction to your answer. Restating the question: 1) makes sure everyone has heard it, 2) makes sure you understand what you are being asked, and 3) gives you a moment to formulate a more effective answer.

6. **Vary the discussion format.** Use pairs, small groups, or large group discussions.

Facilitating Learning Activities

Set-up the activity.

1. **Introduce and briefly explain the activity.** Draw the connection between the topic and the purpose or rationale of the activity. Be sure to cover: 1) step-by-step instructions, 2) materials needed, 3) deliverables to have when finished, and 4) amount of time to complete the activity.

2. **Provide observation points or questions.** Present any set-up questions to help participants observe themselves more closely. For example, you may ask participants to notice what role communication plays in the activity.

3. **Check for understanding.** Make sure everyone understands the directions and what is expected of them before beginning the activity.

Monitor the activity.

1. **Monitor the participants**. Walk around the room to answer questions and to keep participants on track.

2. **Watch for debriefing points.** As participants are working through the activity, watch for incidents and issues, struggles and breakthroughs that can be used in the debriefing the activity.

3. **Give time updates.** Let participants know how much time they have remaining to complete the activity. For example, say, "You have about five minutes left."

Debrief participants after the activity.

The following three questions can be used to conduct a quick and effective debrief.

1. **What happened?** This question brings out different perspectives about what happened during the activity.

2. **So what?** This question highlights the importance of what happened. It is here that participants begin to express their reactions to what happened.

3. **What now?** This question connects ideas together and relates them to other activities and course content. It also introduces action planning. Participants discuss what they will do differently because of what was learned in the activity.

Deliver T-02

Directions: Use this structure, that draws on *Nine Events of Instruction* by Robert Gagne and Leslie Briggs, to organize your presentations and learning activities.

1. **Grab the participants' attention.**
   Not only is it important to make a good first impression, it is also important to gain the participants' attention as soon as possible. <u>Suggestions</u>: Conduct a powerful and attention-gaining mini-activity, provide a thought-provoking statement or rhetorical question, or tell a brief but engaging story or anecdote.

2. **Turn the focus to the learning objective(s).**
   Present your learning objective(s) in a context that matters to participants. <u>Suggestion</u>: Explain to participants how the new knowledge and skill will play out in the work environment. Stress why the learning is critical with real-world examples.

3. **Prompt participants to recall what they already know about this topic.**
   By bringing their relevant knowledge to mind, you can highlight common misconceptions and better relate your content to their point of view. <u>Suggestion</u>: Ask a show-of-hands question or have the audience picture themselves in a situation that directly relates to the topic.

4. **Present the content.**
   Make sure the activity (the presentation, role-play, or case study) is not just active but thought-provoking and focused. <u>Suggestion</u>: Make sure your key points are not obscured by unnecessary information.

5. **Guide participants and point out key features.**
   Emphasize key content and critical decision points by providing prompts, cues, examples, and clues. <u>Suggestion</u>: Do not give away every answer, but let them draw some of their own conclusions.

6. **Provide authentic practice and feedback.**
   Make sure your learning activity is based on realistic practice, situations that are authentic and meaningful to participants. <u>Suggestions</u>: Even with lecture/presentation you can ask thought-provoking questions, provide opportunities for small group discussion, or give the audience a short task to work through in their own minds. Feedback could be given in several ways: instructor-to-participant, participant-to-participant, or participant-to-self (through guided reflection or use of video recording equipment).

7. **Close effectively.**
   Provide a meaningful summary and "learning to learn" debrief. <u>Suggestion</u>: Finish by (a) summarizing key learning – not verbatim but through rephrasing and perhaps a "one last thing to think about" anecdote, and (b) by guiding participants to identify specific instances in the very near future when they can apply what they have just heard to their own personal and professional lives.

Deliver T-03

Directions: Most of us have heard the words of Confucius, "Give them a fish and they eat for a day, teach them to fish and they eat for life." Use these guidelines to build some "learning to fish" into your learning activities.

A. **Define key points or tasks to cover.**

Start by making a list of the key points or tasks you want to cover in each debrief, then look at the various debrief and reflection models below to see how you can integrate the key points into those models.

Remember that your goal is not only for participants to learn these key points, but to discover their own strategies for continuing to learn about these key points and tasks.

B. **Choose debrief and reflection models.**

1. **Basic self-guided learning model**
   Require participants to
   - Explain their views.
   - Defend their positions (especially when challenged by others).
   - Evaluate their ideas and strategies against others'.

2. **In-process debrief**
   - Participants talk through the processes they are taking to complete the activity.
   - Participants determine how well their process is working.
   - If their process is not working as well as expected, they describe how they will compensate for this.

3. **Basic debrief model**
   - What happened?
   - What guiding principles or lessons learned can you derive from this experience?
   - How will these lessons learned affect the way you will act in similar situations?

4. **After action review model**
   - What happened?
   - How is what happened like what you expected?
   - How is it different from what you expected?
   - What will you do next time?
   - When and where exactly is this "next time?"

St. Charles Consulting Group © 2010

Directions: Share these guidelines with your classroom instructors so that they can better help participants build on their strengths and learn from their mistakes.

1. **Base feedback on a model of good performance**. Participants and observers need to agree on what successful performance looks like – what specific behaviors need to be developed. Provide the model of behavior before the practice takes place and refer to the model or standard when delivering feedback. ("You are doing both X and Y, but you're doing Y <u>before</u> X rather than after it.")

2. **Be prompt**. Feedback should immediately follow the performance on which it is based.

3. **Limit feedback**. Focus on priority behaviors. Some instructors or coaches believe that the more feedback they give, the better. This is incorrect. Participants can only absorb and work on a few things at a time. Too much feedback, even if accurate, is confusing and demoralizing.

4. **Decide on the appropriate format**. Weigh both learning and logistical needs to determine the format for feedback. For example, the activity may have a critical and personal nature that requires one-on-one feedback in a breakout room.

5. **Make time for feedback**. Allow time after each skill practice for feedback. For example, a 45-minute activity should have 10 or 15 minutes allotted for feedback. Of course, the amount of time for feedback also depends on whether feedback is one-to-one or one-to-many.

6. **Address only observed behaviors and be descriptive rather than evaluative**. Talk about what you saw or heard, not about what you think you saw or heard. Relate situations and behaviors and encourage participants to draw their own conclusions.

7. **Build on strengths and emphasize the positive**. Point out the positive aspects of participants' skills as something to build on. Turn negatives into positives or opportunities for improvement.

8. **Do not mix criticism with compliments**. Avoid using compliments as a prelude to criticism. Do not add unnecessary, and potentially derogatory, qualifiers to your praise – for example, do not say, "You did fine, considering that this is a new concept to you."

9. **Be honest**. Be honest in your praise and do not overstate an achievement – otherwise you may undermine the sincerity of your other feedback.

10. **Create receptivity**. Do not underestimate the discomfort of a person trying to learn a new skill. Acknowledge the difficulty of the task in the activity set-up, offer encouragement during the activity, and acknowledge successes afterwards.

11. **Accommodate individual differences**. Consider participant characteristics, such as skill level, job level, and experience, and make your feedback appropriate and relevant. Try to "speak their language" by adapting your feedback to things with which they are familiar. Be sensitive to cultural differences when deciding how best to deliver your feedback – for example, in choosing how direct your feedback should be.

12. **Frame your feedback in a broader context.** Provide feedback not only in terms of what happened today but also in terms of what should happen going forward – what behaviors should and should not be part of the participants' on the job skills.

Deliver T-05

Directions: Energizers allow participants to move around, change their focus, and refresh their minds so they can return to core content with renewed vigor. Before teaching a course, look through this list and identify some energizers to "keep in your back pocket" and use when needed. These may seem "hokey" given the sophistication of your audience; however, the basic premise is to introduce some activity which gets people moving and thinking differently. Feel free to come up with your own ideas that arrive at the desired outcome.

The Penny Game

1. Give everyone 10 pennies. Each person must name one thing about himself/herself that is different from everyone else. (For example, an adventurous group member might say, "I have climbed Pikes Peak.")
2. The speaker puts a penny in the middle. If another player has also climbed Pikes Peak, he/she can put in a penny as well.
3. The first person to get rid of all his/her pennies wins.

Two Truths and a Lie

1. Ask participants to write down three statements about themselves – two of the statements must be true and one false.
2. Go around the circle and have each person read his or her three statements. Then, have the others try and guess which the false statement is.
3. Consider awarding a small prize to those who are able to fool the other group members.

Weather Report

1. Go around the circle, beginning with the leader, and describe how you are feeling right now in terms of a weather report – for example, partly cloudy, sunny. The leader should set the example for depth.
2. Participants can explain why they chose that type of weather.

Group Climate Survey

1. Draw a five-point scale on a flipchart. Label the 1 "Totally disagree," the 3 "Neutral," and the 5 "Totally agree."
2. Write a series of thought-provoking statements related to the course on a flipchart and ask each participant to pick a number of where he or she stands on each statement.

Bodyguard

1. Ask everyone to stand up and clear an area for them all to walk quickly around in.
2. Explain that each person is a VIP who needs protecting.
3. Ask everyone to identify (without telling anyone) someone in the room who will be their bodyguard and someone else in the room who is an assassin.
4. Explain that when you say go you want them to keep the bodyguard between themselves and their assassin at all times.
5. Say "Go!"

Jeopardy

1. Facilitator uses a Jeopardy game format by jotting down some questions on 5x7 index cards and taping each into a Jeopardy grid drawn on a flipchart. Divide participants into teams. Rather than having teams signal in to answer, allow each team's spokesperson to choose a question category and give that team 1 minute to discuss their answer (the spokesperson answers).

———— CONTINUED ———————— **Deliver T-06**

Personal Profile

1. Give participants index cards and ask them to write a response to one (or more) of the items below. Ask participants as a group to share responses or have participants stand up and network individually, introducing themselves and sharing their responses.
   - My greatest achievement
   - Three things that matter most to me
   - Three things I do well
   - Three things I would like to learn to do well
   - Personal motto by which I try to live
   - One thing I would like to have said about me
   - Two people I would most like to have dinner with

Listening to Both Sides

1. Have groups divide into threes.
2. Designate one person to be the observer. Have that pick a personal dilemma (for example, to take a vacation or keep working).
3. The two others in the group must each pick one side of the dilemma to argue. They should debate the issue as strongly as possible. Let this go on about two minutes.
4. Rotate roles so that each person gets the opportunity to be the observer.
5. Debrief by asking how it felt to hear your own internal dilemma argued "externally"? How convincing were the arguments? The learning point is that we typically only listen to the side with which we are most comfortable.

What Can This be Used for?

1. Hang an object from the ceiling of the training room (pencil, slinky, etc.). Sit in a circle and ask the person to your right to think of a unique usage for the hanging item. As you proceed around the circle, each person must think of a use not previously given. Instead of simply going around the circle, you may want to incorporate a ball into the icebreaker, which a person must throw to the next person who will speak.

Gallery Walk Add-on

1. Write an open-ended question on the top of five flipchart sheets. Post each sheet in different parts of the room. Participants walk by each flipchart, quickly write their response, and then move on.

Cinquains (pronounced 'SIN canes')

1. Participants work in pairs to write a poem on a subject related to the course in the following format: first line, one noun; second line, two adjectives or adverbs; third line, four verbs; fourth line, four word phrase; fifth line, one noun. (Guide participants by writing this format on a flipchart.)

Stepping Stones

1. Ask participants to write their responses to this question: "What 3 major stepping stones – events or decisions – have lead you to where you are today?" Allow 5 minutes.
2. Ask participants to find a partner and share their "stepping stones" for 10 minutes. One person tells the other his or her stepping-stones for 5 minutes, and then they switch roles.
3. Debrief by asking the group the following:
   - What patterns did you notice in your stepping stones?
   - What do you think your next stepping stone will be?

Deliver T-06

CPE FIELD GUIDE ———————— CPE Attendance Record

Directions: Use this form to document attendance at a live training event for CPE purposes.

Course Name: _____

Sponsor: _____   Date: _____

Facility: _____   Start Time: _____

Location: _____   End Time: _____

Lead Instructor: _____   Max CPE Credits: _____

Participant Name (printed)	Participant Signature	Time In	Time Out

Page: _____

Deliver T-07

Document

CPE Certi | Compliance Checklist
Participant List
Program Evaluation

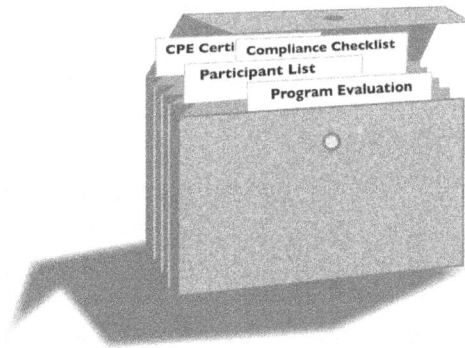

Organizing is what you do before you do something,
so that when you do it, it is not all mixed up.

— A.A. Milne *(Author of Winnie the Pooh)*

CPE FIELD GUIDE ———————— Participant Evaluation Form

Directions: Use this form to gather feedback from participants on various aspects of the CPE program.

Course Name: _____ Date(s): _____

Please indicate the extent to which you agree with the following statements using a scale of 1 to 10 (where "1" is "totally <u>disagree</u>" and "10" is "totally <u>agree</u>"):

1. The learning objectives of this program were clearly communicated.
2. The learning objectives of this program were met.
3. The stated prerequisites were appropriate. (Enter "0" if there were no prerequisites.)
4. The pre-work contributed to the learning experience. (Enter "0" if no pre-work was assigned.)
5. The program materials were accurate. (Enter "0" if there were no materials.)
6. The program materials were relevant and helped to meet the learning objectives.
7. Audio and video materials were effective. (Enter "0" if audio and video materials were not used.)
8. The physical environment for training, including technology, was conducive to effective learning.
9. In general, the content of the program was timely and relevant to me.
10. Overall, the program did a good job of enhancing my knowledge and skill.
11. I would recommend this program to others.
12. To what extent did you understand the concepts presented <u>prior</u> to this program?

    ❏ Not at all   ❏ Only slightly   ❏ Somewhat   ❏ For the most part   ❏ Very much so

13. To what extent did you understand the concepts presented <u>after</u> the program?

    ❏ Not at all   ❏ Only slightly   ❏ Somewhat   ❏ For the most part   ❏ Very much so

14. How would you rate the amount of time allotted for the program?

    ❏ Not enough time   ❏ Right amount of time   ❏ Too much time

What letter grade – from A (excellent) **to F** (failed), **including pluses and minuses – would you give to each of the instructors in terms of their effectiveness in the role?**

15a. Instructor (name): _____
15b. Instructor (name): _____
15c. Instructor (name): _____

In what ways do you think the program could have been improved?

——————————————— **Document T-01** —

Directions: Use this form to gather feedback from instructors on various aspects of the CPE program.

Course Name: _____   **Date(s):** _____

Please indicate the extent to which you agree with the following statements using a scale of 1 to 10 (where "1" is "totally disagree" and "10" is "totally agree"):

1. Overall, the structure of the program – in terms of topics, the sequencing of topics, and the amount of time devoted to each – was well designed.   ☐

2. Overall, the instructional content was well compiled and packaged.   ☐

3. Support materials (slides, handouts, instructor notes, etc.) were adequate for conveying the instructional content.   ☐

4. Support materials were provided sufficiently in advance to allow for appropriate preparation.   ☐

5. In general, the content of the program was timely, relevant, and at the right level for the participants.   ☐

6. Participants were appropriately prepared when they came to the session.   ☐

7. Participants were involved and engaged throughout the program.   ☐

8. Participants were respectful of the process and worked well with others.   ☐

9. Co-instructors managed the program flow effectively. (Enter "0" if there were not co-instructors.)   ☐

10. On-site staff resources provided excellent responsiveness and support.   ☐

11. The physical environment for the training was conducive to effective learning.   ☐

If you were to teach this material again, what would you suggest be done differently to improve the program?

_____   _____
Instructor (name)   Date

Document T-02

Directions: Use this template if participants need a record evidencing completion of a CPE program.

Certificate of Completion

Sponsor Name
Sponsor Address & Phone Number

This certificate is presented to:

PARTICIPANT NAME

for satisfactory of completion of:

COURSE NAME

CPE credits have been earned as follows:

Field of Study	CPE Credits
Field of Study 1	##.#
Field of Study 2	##.#
Field of Study 3	##.#
Field of Study 4	##.#
Total CPE Credits	##.#

Number of credits eligible for:		
	Ethics	
	Employee Benefits	
	Fraud	
	SEC	
	Yellow Book (A&A)	
	Yellow Book (Government)	

The method of instructional delivery was [group-live, group internet-based, or self-study].

The program took place at:

Facility Name – City, State, Zipcode

Date(s): Month ##, 201x

Approved by: _____
CPE Administrator

Document T-03

CPE FIELD GUIDE ———————— Instructor CPE Submittal Form

Directions: Have your instructors use this form to report time spent on a CPE program.

Instructor: _____

Course Name: _____   **Date(s):** _____

An instructor can claim credit for <u>actual</u> time spent in instruction and for <u>actual</u> time spent in preparation (up to 2 times the amount of instruction time) but ONLY: 1) <u>if</u> this is the first time the instructor has taught this material, or 2) <u>if</u> the material has been substantially revised since the previous presentation. (**Note**: Some states have set limits on the amount of instructor CPE that can be counted. CPAs should check with their regulatory bodies.)

Topic(s) taught:

_____

_____

_____

_____

Hours spent in PREPARATION (rounded down to nearest half hour):

Hours spent in INSTRUCTION (rounded down to nearest half hour):

This is the first time that I have taught this material.   ❏ Yes   ❏ No

I have taught on this topic in the past, but the material has been substantially revised.   ❏ Yes   ❏ No

Instructor Signature: _____   Date: _____

———————————————————————— **Document T-04**

St. Charles Consulting Group
© 2010

Directions: Use this template if instructors need a record evidencing involvement in a CPE program.

Certificate of Completion

Sponsor Name
Sponsor Address & Phone Number

This certificate is presented to:

INSTRUCTOR NAME

for satisfactory instruction of:

COURSE NAME

CPE credits have been earned as follows:

Field of Study	CPE Credits
Field of Study 1	##.#
Field of Study 2	##.#
Field of Study 3	##.#
Field of Study 4	##.#
Total CPE Credits	##.#

Number of credits eligible for:		
	Ethics	
	Employee Benefits	
	Fraud	
	SEC	
	Yellow Book (A&A)	
	Yellow Book (Government)	

The method of instructional delivery was [group-live, group internet-based, or self-study].

The program took place at:

Facility Name – City, State, Zipcode

Date(s): Month ##, 201x

Approved by: _____
                           CPE Administrator

Note: Some states may set limits on the amount of instructor CPE that can be counted.
CPAs should check with their regulatory bodies.

Document T-05

CPE FIELD GUIDE ——— Author/Developer CPE Submittal Form

Directions: Have your authors and course developers use this form to report time spent on a qualifying CPE publication. To qualify, the article, book, or CPE program must be formally reviewed by a publisher or other independent party. CPE credits should be claimed only upon publication/completion.

Author/Developer: _____

Publication/Completion Date: _____

Publication/Course Title: _____

Publication/Course Type: ☐ Article ☐ Book ☐ CPE Program ☐ Other: _____

Publisher or Independent Reviewer: _____

Contact Information – Email: _____ Phone: _____

Description of Development Impact
(how publication increased the professional competence of the author/developer):

Hours Spent: **CPE Field(s) of Study:**

_____   _____

_____   _____

_____   _____

_____   _____

Author/Developer Signature: _____   **Date:** _____

Note: Attach a copy of the) that names the writer as author or contributor.

Document T-06

Directions: Use this template if authors/developers need a record evidencing involvement in a CPE program.

Certificate of Completion

Sponsor Name
Sponsor Address & Phone Number

This certificate is presented to:

<u>AUTHOR/DEVELOPER NAME</u>

for satisfactory publication of:

PUBLICATION OR COURSE NAME

CPE credits have been earned as follows:

Field of Study	CPE Credits
Field of Study 1	##.#
Field of Study 2	##.#
Field of Study 3	##.#
Field of Study 4	##.#
Total CPE Credits	##.#

Number of credits eligible for:

Ethics	
Employee Benefits	
Fraud	
SEC	
Yellow Book (A&A)	
Yellow Book (Government)	

The publication was published by PUBLISHER on DATE.
OR
The CPE course was completed on DATE.

Approved by: _____
CPE Administrator

Note: Some states may set limits on the amount of publication CPE that can be counted.
CPAs should check with their regulatory bodies.

Document T-07

Directions: Use this form to document all of the key elements of the program – from design & development through to delivery – for CPE purposes.

Course Name: _____   **Date(s):** _____

Design of Learning Activities

❑ The learning activities were based on relevant learning objectives and outcomes that clearly articulated the knowledge, skills, and abilities that can be achieved by participants.

❑ Learning activities were developed and executed in a manner consistent with the prerequisite education, experience, and/or advance preparation of participants.

❑ Activities, materials, and delivery methods were current, technically accurate, and effectively designed.

❑ Learning activities were developed by individuals or teams having expertise in the subject matter, as demonstrated through practical experience or education.

❑ Learning activities were reviewed by qualified persons other than those who developed them to assure that the program is technically accurate and current and addresses the stated learning objectives.

❑ This content review occurred before the first presentation of these materials or a significant revision of the CPE program.

Descriptive Materials

❑ Descriptive materials were provided in a timely manner in advance that enabled potential participants to assess the appropriateness of learning activities to their professional competence development needs.

❑ The descriptive material included:
  – Learning objectives
  – Prerequisites
  – Program level (basic, intermediate, advanced, update, and overview)
  – Program content
  – Advance preparation
  – Instructional delivery methods
  – Recommended CPE credit
  – Course registration requirements

❑ The prerequisite education, experience, and/or advance preparation, if any, were clearly identified in precise language so that potential participants could readily ascertain whether they qualify for the program.

Program Delivery

❑ Learning activities were presented in a manner consistent with the descriptive and technical materials provided.

❑ Instructors were competent and current in the subject matter, skilled in the use of the appropriate instructional methods and technology, and prepared in advance.

❑ The instructor's performance was evaluated at the conclusion of the program to determine the instructor's suitability to serve in the future.

———— CONTINUED ———— **Document T-08**

Program Delivery (continued)

❑ Evaluations were solicited from participants and instructors to determine whether:
- Stated learning objectives were met.
- Prerequisite requirements were appropriate (if applicable).
- Program materials were accurate.
- Program materials were relevant and contributed to the achievement of the learning
- objectives.
- Instructional methods employed were appropriate and effective.
- Time allotted to the learning activity was appropriate.
- Individual instructors were effective (if applicable).
- Facilities and/or technological equipment was appropriate.
- Handout or advance preparation materials were satisfactory.
- Audio and video materials were effective.

❑ Evaluation results to assess program effectiveness were shared with the program developer(s) and instructor(s).

CPE Credit

❑ CPE credits were determined on the basis of one 50-minute period equaling one CPE credit. One-half CPE credit increments (equal to 25 minutes) were permitted after the first credit had been earned in a given learning activity. If the total minutes of a sponsored learning activity were greater than 50, but not equally divisible by 50, the CPE credits granted were rounded down to the nearest one-half credit.

❑ CPE credits were assigned to the appropriate field(s) of study.

❑ Instructors of the learning activities were given the opportunity to receive CPE credit for both their preparation and presentation time to the extent the activities maintain or improve their professional competence and meet the requirements of these CPE standards. (Instructors are eligible for actual preparation time up to two times the number of CPE credits to which participants would be entitled, in addition to the time for presentation.)

❑ Developers of the learning activities were given the opportunity to receive CPE credit for their research and writing time to the extent it maintained or improved their professional competence.

❑ Documentation was provided to program participants with to demonstrate program completion that included:
- CPE program sponsor name and contact information
- Participant's name
- Course title
- Course field(s) of study
- Date offered or completed
- Location (if applicable)
- Type of instructional/delivery method used
- Amount of CPE credit recommended
- Verification by CPE program sponsor representative

Document Retention

☐ Documentation will be retained for five years* to evidence compliance with CPE standards that includes, but may not be limited to:
- Records of participation
- Dates and locations
- Instructor names and credentials
- Number of CPE credits earned by participants
- Results of program evaluations
- Copies of program materials
- Evidence that the program materials were developed and reviewed by qualified parties
- A record of how CPE credits were determined

* - In California, the document retention period is six years.

Document T-08

Directions: Use this guidance to organize the archive file and to officially closedown the CPE program.

Course Name: _____ **Date(s):** _____

The closedown process is mostly about creating an organized archive file so that compliance with the CPE standards can be evidenced and supported for at least 5 years.* As shown in the previous tool – the **Conformation of Compliance Checklist** (Document T-08) – this archive file should minimally contain the information that follows. (Note that the relevant tools from this guide are shown in parentheses):

- ❑ Records of participation (**CPE Attendance Record** – Deliver T-07)
- ❑ Dates and locations (**CPE Attendance Record** – Deliver T-07)
- ❑ Instructor names and credentials (**Instructor Team Profile** – Deliver T-01)
- ❑ Number of CPE credits earned by participants and a record of how CPE credits were determined (**CPE Calculation Template** – Develop T-12)
- ❑ Results of program evaluations (summary of data collected using **Participant Evaluation Form** – Document T-01 and **Instructor Evaluation Form** – Document T-02)
- ❑ Copies of program materials (referencing the **Learning Materials Menu** – Develop T-02)
- ❑ Evidence that the program materials were developed and reviewed by qualified parties (the **Development Team Profile** – Develop T-01, the **Developer Review Form** – Develop T-09, and the **Technical Review Form** – Develop T-10)

To create an even more complete record, it is advised that the following items also be included in the closedown file (if they were created as part of the program creation process):

- ❑ Course description (reference **Course Description Tool** – Design T-10)
- ❑ Master design document (reference **Master Design Document Template** – Design T-11)
- ❑ Samples of CPE certificates issued (reference **CPE Certificate** tools – Document T-03 through T-07)
- ❑ Confirmation of Compliance (**Confirmation of Compliance Checklist** – Document T-08)

Other actions to be included in the closedown process include:

- ❑ Sharing program results with sponsors and other interested stakeholders.
- ❑ Sharing evaluation results with the developer and instructor teams and document improvements that should be made in the next program update.
- ❑ Maintaining an indication of when and under what conditions the program materials should be reviewed and updated.

Note: The archive file need not be maintained in hardcopy. In fact, there are a number of benefits of having the information stored in electronic data files, assuming that the files are secure and systematically backed up.

* - In California, the document retention period is six years.

Document T-09

About the Authors

Ross Stern

Ross Stern is an experienced professional known for implementing strategic initiatives through design, development, and management of innovative training & human capital programs. Most recently, he led a large-scale rollout of a new practice methodology for a leading professional services firm – just one example of his success with large, complex engagements.

Ross joined St. Charles in 2007 following five years as the Director of Training for Parson Consulting – a global consulting firm serving corporate CFOs. In this capacity, Ross was responsible for developing the firm's internal training strategy and curriculum and for managing the firm's CPE policies and procedures.

Prior to that, Ross spent 20 years with Arthur Andersen, serving in roles that included Director of Training for multiple service lines, where he led the training development groups responsible for aligning the business and education strategies. He also served on the Andersen Human Capital Executive Council, providing strategic direction on global human resource initiatives. In his last role with Andersen, before its dissolution, Ross was the Director of Human Resources for the Learning and Personal Growth practice in St. Charles. In this capacity, Ross implemented a comprehensive performance review system and directed the internal professional development program. Over the years, he effectively managed significant change during periods of dramatic growth within the firm's global training function.

Contact Ross at rstern@stccg.com.

Rod Mebane

Rod Mebane is a seasoned professional who specializes in corporate learning strategy with an emphasis on executive and leadership development. Rod's expertise has both depth and breadth across learning which gives him an ability to integrate strategic business objectives into all areas of professional development. Rod's capabilities in the areas of organizational communication, strategic facilitation, and change planning and implementation have led to his success in driving results for his clients.

Before joining St. Charles in 2006, Rod served as the Chief Learning Officer at BDO Seidman – the nation's seventh largest public accounting firm. While there, Rod designed and implemented a comprehensive learning framework, introduced competency-based performance systems, and infused management development throughout the CPE curriculum. In his seven years at BDO, he oversaw the development and delivery of dozens of CPE programs in audit & accounting, tax, and consulting. He also implemented a firm-wide CPE compliance process and was responsible for BDO joining NASBA's national registry of CPE sponsors.

Prior to BDO, Rod served as Senior Performance Consultant and Director at Arthur Andersen where he provided knowledge management support to executive firm leadership on global strategy and performance management initiatives. He is broadly published on a variety of learning and general business topics.

Contact Rod at rmebane@stccg.com.

Notes

Notes

Help Improve the CPE Field Guide

Let us know how the **CPE Field Guide** can be revised, reworked, extended and renewed with your creative improvement suggestions. Please use the space below to describe the things that you think should be changed and the additions that you think should be made.

_____

_____

_____

_____

_____

_____

_____

_____

_____

_____

_____

_____

_____

_____

ALSO … If you have content that you feel could be a valuable part of the **CPE Field Guide** and are willing to have it included (without royalty interests), please pass it along, and we will be happy to list you as a vital contributor to the **Guide** in future editions.

SEND … your information to:

St. Charles Publications
An Activity of the St. Charles Consulting Group
1121 E. Main St., Suite 220
St. Charles, IL 60174

OR … email your reactions and suggestions to: **PUBLISHER@STCHARLESPUBLICATIONS.COM**

THANK YOU FOR YOUR INTEREST AND SUPPORT!